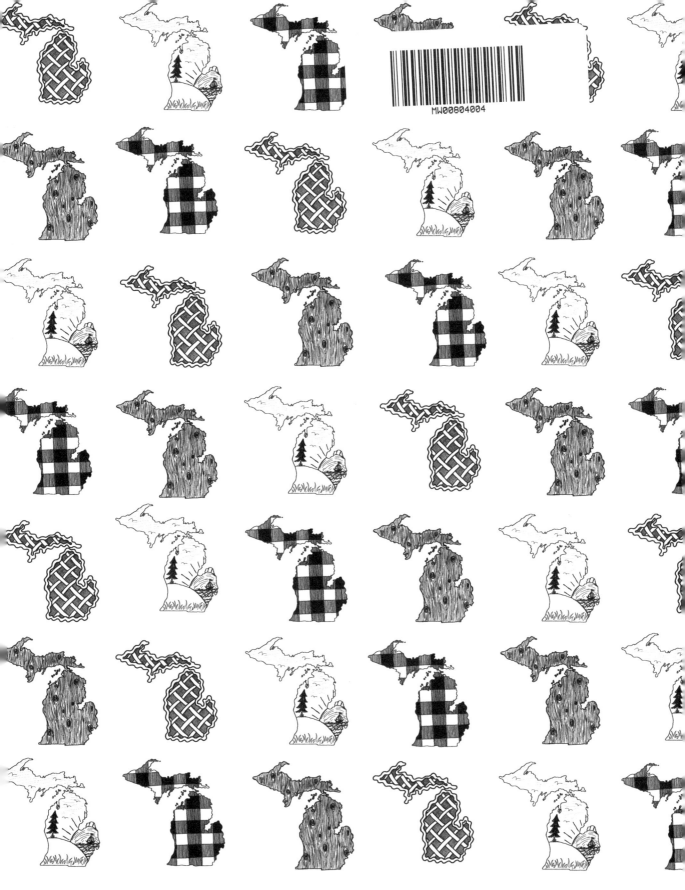

MW00804004

-MY LITTLE MICHIGAN KITCHEN-

recipes and stories from a homemade life lived well

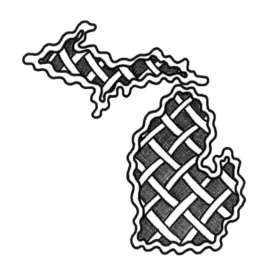

Mandy McGovern

Kitchen Joy Press

MY LITTLE MICHIGAN KITCHEN

My Little Michigan Kitchen, recipes and stories from a homemade life lived well by Mandy McGovern

Requests for information should be addressed to:

Kitchen Joy Press 887 Bailey Park Drive NE, Grand Rapids, MI 49525.

ISBN-13: 978-0-578-44496-3

ISBN-10: 0-578-44496-8

Library of Congress Control Number: 2019900317

First Edition. Fourth Printing. July 2020.

Printed in China.

Cover design: Mandy McGovern

All photography by Mandy McGovern with the exception of the following:

Front cover photo: Michael McGovern

Pgs. v, 116, 241 by Michael McGovern

Pgs. xiv, xv, xviii, xix, 18-19, 58, 84-85, 164-165, 179, 208-209, 214, 220-221, 249, 260-263 by Robin L. Smith

Headshot pg. 196 by Alex Rathbun, photographer. BrightlyAlex.com

Headshot pg. 260 by Missie McGovern.

All illustrations and artwork by Mandy McGovern.

Book design and typeset by Mandy McGovern.

Kitchen Joy® is a registered trademark of Amanda McGovern.

FOR MICHAEL, ADDILYN, AND AMELIA.

YOU BREATHE LIFE INTO MY DREAMS AND ADVENTURE INTO MY SOUL.

ALL MY LOVE ALWAYS.

This is my invariable advice to people: learn how to cook—try new recipes, learn from your mistakes, be fearless, and above all have fun.

–Julia Child

CONTENTS

Introduction

Hi there! Thanks for picking up my book. I hope you find something you enjoy within these pages.

When people hear that I've been creating my own cookbook, I've often been asked what made me choose to take on such a project. In short, my heart didn't give me a choice. It's just something I needed to do, so here it is. The fact that anyone might read it is just icing on the cake.

The seed for this cookbook was planted in my mind as a young newlywed who was craving the knowledge needed to create a variety of meals for my new husband. As a young couple, we adventured together near and far whenever our schedules and bank account would allow. We had been bitten by the travel bug and relished any sort of getaway that we could manage. We were college students, homeowners, and best friends. I quickly adopted the tradition (some might say compulsion) of collecting a cookbook from each place we visited. I sought out books that focused on the local cuisine and history of the food culture from each of our destinations. My shelves quickly filled with a wide variety of beautiful reminders of our adventures, and the incredible meals we enjoyed on our journeys. Some books were huge, colorful hardcover masterpieces with hundreds of recipes ranging from simple to nearly impossible to recreate at home due to the exotic ingredients required. Some were thin paperbacks that didn't catch one's eye for its flashy photography or professional illustrations, but were bursting with charming tales of a life lived deliciously and recipes that were understated and decidedly un-fancy, but represented the food history of that region perfectly. Having been born and raised in Michigan, **my heart and soul beat with joy for the beloved state that is shaped like a mitten.** Imagine my disappointment when I scoured shop after shop in dozens of towns only to find that either no such Michigan cookbook existed, or at the very least it was not readily available. Souvenir fail.

After a decade of marriage and adventures with Michael, my fearless companion and partner in crime, I had accumulated an arsenal of food knowledge and experience in the kitchen that made me just crazy enough to think that I should create the book I had been searching for over the years. Food history, cooking techniques, the science and chemistry of baking, the personal yet communal experience of enjoying a shared meal, the memories triggered by a certain taste or smell, all of it engulfed my curiosity and took my life in an entirely new and more passionate direction. I started my blog, Kitchen Joy, in 2013 as a way to chronicle my food adventures in and out of the kitchen. My tagline that I gave my blog on that very first day of my internet existence was "Culinary adventures in my little Michigan kitchen". It's definitely been an adventure, and it just gets better and better!

I cooked my way through dozens of the cookbooks in my collection in those early days, choosing a "cookbook of the week" to focus on and cooking all of our meals from that particular book every day for the week before moving on to the next book. It forced me to introduce a variety of new preparations and ingredients that I might not have adopted so quickly on my own. It was my version of a very basic cooking school experience. I moved on to more difficult techniques, working my way through the coursebooks from Le Cordon Bleu's culinary and patisserie programs. I took cake decorating classes and made wedding cakes in my tiny kitchen that had about 2 feet of counterspace, 1 drawer, and no dishwasher. I took orders for elaborately decorated cakes and sugar cookies to commemorate birthdays, weddings, graduations, Christmas, you name it.

That kitchen, the tiny one in our very first home with the purple door adorned with pretty white lettering spelling "Hello" to all who entered, was the stage for my transformation into full-blown food nerd. Bless his heart, my husband was an eager supporter, taste tester, and dishwasher.

Over the years, my blog has morphed into a much more personal expression of who I am. It is a place that I share stories and original recipes that are near and dear to my heart. Where I swoon over ingredients that are in season, or I wax nostalgic over a pastry enjoyed while traveling. We even lived in Italy for a while and I got to take my little blogging gig on the road!

It wasn't until we had seen and done more than we ever had imagined we would in those first years of marriage that we realized our absolute favorite place, for the scenery, activities, food, and more, is good ol' Michigan. Our home state that has more to offer than visitors might realize, and it was right under our noses the whole time. We took a leap of faith and bought ourselves a cute little cabin "up North" in northern lower Michigan. Not to be confused with the purist's definition of "up north", which is the U.P. (Upper Peninsula). After that we really settled into our best life. Hiking, fishing, cooking, campfires, day trips to charming little waterfront towns, farmers markets, bakeries, all of it opened our eyes and hearts to this spectacular place more than ever before.

Early Summer 2016 brought us yet another adventure. We finally received our dream of giving birth to a healthy baby. Sweet Addilyn Joy was an adventurer from day one. Her favorite food at age one was sushi. The good, expensive, spicy stuff. She makes her parents very proud with her excitement about new flavors. I'm still coming to grips with the realization that the only food that she truly cannot tolerate is....potatoes. What? It's true. Pickled ginger? She's all about it. French fries, mashed potatoes, or baked potatoes? Not a chance.

It was in those first weeks of motherhood that I began to reimagine my future. I was not only a brand new mom, but for the first time in ten years, I no longer worked a full-time day job. I was suddenly a stay-at-home mom, whatever that meant. In between diapers, feedings, tummy time, and story books, **I found myself wondering if I had what it took to pursue my cookbook dream.** I kept my plans to myself at first, while I spent baby's naptimes doing research into the cookbook writing and publishing process. Could I do it? I didn't know, but I did know that I needed to try.

If I can teach my daughters a few things over the course of my life, I hope they learn from example to work hard and give your very best effort to achieve your dreams. To **find joy** in the process of chasing your goals with passion and curiosity, even if the outcome isn't quite what you had envisioned from the start. Don't be afraid to fail. Don't live with regret for not trying. Go for it. Embrace your hobbies and pursue them feverishly.

I will never forget those days spent testing recipes and taking photos while wearing Addilyn in a carrier on my chest. She is such a huge part of this journey and I will cherish those memories for the rest of my life.

Two years later, in the Summer of 2018, baby sister Amelia Joy arrived. We were about halfway through the book-writing process at that point, and given the fact that pregnancy aversions prevented me from recipe-testing for several months, along with having moved to a different house, I was twitching with desire to get back to work on this project that occupied such a big piece of my heart. Little Millie spent countless hours cuddling on my lap while I typed away at this book, laid on a blanket next to me as I took photos of recipes, and even though she has only tasted a few of its recipes, she's every bit as much part of this book as I am.

This book is nothing groundbreaking, intentionally so. It is a love story to Michigan.

It is a collection of recipes that are part of the fiber that makes up our family and our home.

It is a keepsake for my daughters to cherish when they're older and they wonder what their Mama did all day as a stay-at-home mom. It is a scrapbook of adventures, a series of postcard-worthy photos from a state where the slogan is "If you seek a pleasant peninsula, look about you." The state whose Pure Michigan TV commercials bring tears to the eyes of Michiganders the world over. It is a menagerie of sights and flavors that will hopefully inspire readers to visit Michigan, seek out fresh produce, source local ingredients, and enjoy a homemade life lived well.

Welcome to My little Michigan kitchen. let's be friends.

-Mandy

If you seek a pleasant peninsula, look about you.
—State Motto

Point Betsie Lighthouse- Frankfort , Michigan

Before You Use this Book...

I want you to succeed when you create these recipes at home. These are the measurement methods and exact ingredients used for the development of the recipes in this book. See page 248 for Ingredient Sources.

Measuring Dry ingredients:

Standard cups and spoons- Fluff, scoop, level with knife. Do not tap cups to let ingredients settle.

By weight- gram conversions are provided on pg. 244. This is a more accurate method for measuring ingredients, and also saves on dishes to wash!

Measuring liquid ingredients:

Liquid measuring cups such as Pyrex or beaker-style.

Temperatures:

Oven Temperatures are listed in Fahrenheit. For a Celsius conversion table, (See pg. 244)

A digital instant-read thermometer is necessary for several recipes in this book.

Ingredients used in the recipe development of this book.

All-Purpose Flour: Gold Medal Brand. Results may vary depending on brand of flour used due to differing protein content.

Brown Sugar: All brown sugar listed in this book refers to light brown sugar unless otherwise noted. When measuring brown sugar, always pack it firmly into the measuring cup.

Granulated sugar: Beet sugar vs. Cane sugar (Both can be used interchangeably in the recipes in this book.)

Unsalted butter: All butter listed in this book refers to unsalted butter.

Pure vanilla extract: Absolutely no imitation vanilla is recommended for these recipes. Good quality pure vanilla extract can be found in most major supermarkets, specialty food markets, or online.

Kosher salt: Diamond Crystal brand kosher salt is my go-to kosher salt. If you use Mortons' (NOT recommended), you will need to decrease the amount by about half, and then season to taste. Morton's has a very overpoweringly salty aftertaste as opposed to Diamond Crystals' ability to enhance the flavors of the ingredients without overpowering them.

Dairy products: For best results, use full fat dairy products such as whole milk, sour cream, ricotta, etc. Lowfat or nonfat dairy items affect the texture and flavor of the dish.

Produce: Whenever possible, I recommend using fresh, in-season, local fruits and vegetables. If fresh isn't available to you, frozen is a suitable substitute. None of the recipes in this book have been tested with canned fruits or vegetables, unless otherwise specified.

Maple syrup: Pure Maple Syrup, Grade A Dark Amber/Robust or Grade B are recommended for the recipes in this book. Michigan Maple Syrup is my preference, but Vermont and Canada Maple Syrup are typically easier to source for those outside of Michigan.

Cocoa/Chocolate: Ghirardelli brand cocoa and chocolate were used in the recipe development of this book. 100% unsweetened cacao, and 100% unsweetened chocolate bars are recommended, especially for Mackinac Island Fudge (Pg.160)

Eggs: All eggs listed in recipes are large eggs.

Cinnamon: Penzey's Spices Vietnamese Cinnamon is my very favorite cinnamon, and it was the only cinnamon used in the recipe development of this book. If using a more generic ground cinnamon, you may need to use a little bit more than listed in the recipe to achieve the intended flavor, as the Vietnamese Cinnamon is fairly strong.

Pepper: I always recommend freshly ground black pepper for its flavor, instead pre-ground pepper.

Yeast: Red Star Platinum Instant Yeast was used in the development of the recipes in this book.

Liquid Smoke: Stubb's Hickory Liquid Smoke is the best tasting liquid smoke I found during my research and recipe testing. It can be purchased on Amazon.com.

Recommended Tools:

The following items are used throughout this book and in my home kitchen on a daily basis:

Whisk	Nonstick skillet
Wooden spatula	Silicone spatulas
Bench scraper	Kitchen Aid or similar stand mixer
Digital instant read thermometer	Fine mesh sieve
Enameled Cast iron Dutch oven	Knives (chef, paring, serrated, bread)
Cast iron skillet	Wood cutting board
Half sheet pans	Silpat baking mats
Pastry Brush	Parchment paper
Food processor	Pastry cutter
Rolling pin	Pie plates
Large stock pot	Springform pan
Heavy-bottomed saucepans	Bundt Pan

"*All happiness depends on a leisurely breakfast.*"

–John Gunther

Breakfast & Brunch

Cinnamon Chip Scones	3
Oatmeal Buttermilk Pancakes	4
Blueberry Muffins	7
Biscuits and Sausage Gravy	8
Turkey Sausage	10
Hot Cross Buns	13
Bran Muffins	17
Sour Cream Waffles	20
Blueberry Dutch Baby	23
Monkey Bread	24
Deep Dish Quiche	26
Pumpkin Donuts	29
Breakfast Burritos	33
Bacon and Corn Breakfast Galette	34
Malted Pancakes	36

Cinnamon Chip Scones

Warm, fluffy wedges of pastry packed with little pops of spice. No eggs, no chilling, and no gadgets. These scones will be your new best friend when you want to impress your guests with very little effort. It'll be our little secret.

3 cups all-purpose flour

2 ½ teaspoons baking powder

1 teaspoon salt

⅓ cup granulated sugar

1 teaspoon cinnamon

½ cup unsalted butter, cubed and chilled

1 ½ cups heavy cream, plus more for brushing

2 teaspoons pure vanilla extract

1 cup Hershey's cinnamon chips

Preheat oven to 400°F.

In a large mixing bowl, whisk together the flour, baking powder, salt, sugar, and cinnamon. Cut in butter using a pastry blender or a fork until lumps are about the size of a pea. Add cream and vanilla, mixing just until combined. Fold in cinnamon chips.

Transfer dough to a lightly floured surface and shape into a large circle about 1-inch thick. Cut into 8 wedges. Arrange wedges on a parchment-lined baking sheet and brush tops with heavy cream.

Bake at 400°F for 16-17 minutes, until golden.

Note: Store in an airtight container at room temperature for up to 3 days. To reheat: Preheat oven to 350°F. Place scones on baking sheet and heat for 6-7 minutes or until warmed through.

Oatmeal Buttermilk Pancakes

The addition of oatmeal in this recipe makes for a rich, flavorful breakfast that will leave you swearing off boxed mixes forever. The buttermilk provides moisture and a hint of tang that complements pure Michigan maple syrup splendidly. Or spread some Nutella and sliced bananas between two pancakes and make a sandwich that will change your life. Choose your own adventure. Also, you're welcome.

½ cup old-fashioned oats

1 ¾ cups all-purpose flour

1 tablespoon baking powder

½ teaspoon baking soda

¼ teaspoon salt

3 tablespoons unsalted butter, cubed and chilled

2 cups buttermilk

1 egg, lightly beaten

Canola oil for pan

Pulse oats in a food processor until they resemble breadcrumbs. Add flour, baking powder, baking soda, and salt to the bowl of the food processor. Pulse to combine. Add butter and pulse until only very small bits of butter remain. Transfer mixture to a large mixing bowl.

In a small bowl, whisk the buttermilk and egg together. Pour into the flour mixture and stir until just moistened.

Heat a tablespoon of oil in a nonstick or cast iron skillet over medium heat. Scoop batter in about ⅓ cup portions, cooking about 3 minutes on the first side, and 2 minutes on the second side, until golden. Repeat with remaining batter.

Makes about ten 6-8" pancakes.

Blueberry Muffins

As a little girl growing up in Michigan, we had some bitter cold Winters. No complaints here though, snow days are the best! I remember many an icy day when my brother and I would gather at the dinner table and have spaghetti, lasagna, or goulash and my mom would serve blueberry muffins alongside our meal. To this day, I still love blueberry muffins with tomato-based main courses. These are my version of blueberry muffins that are suitable for any time of day.

10 tablespoons unsalted butter, melted

1 cup granulated sugar

1 ½ cups sour cream

2 large eggs

2 teaspoons pure vanilla extract

3 teaspoons baking powder

½ teaspoon baking soda

½ teaspoon salt

½ teaspoon cinnamon

Pinch of nutmeg

3 cups all-purpose flour

2 ½-3 cups fresh blueberries

¼ cup raw sugar, for sprinkling

Preheat oven to 375°F. Line 12 cup muffin pan with paper liners.

In a large bowl, whisk together the melted butter, sugar, sour cream, eggs, and vanilla until smooth. Add baking powder, baking soda, salt, cinnamon, and nutmeg. Whisk until combined.

Gently stir in the flour and blueberries. Batter will be thick.

Divide into muffin cups and sprinkle with raw sugar.

Bake 25-30 minutes until golden. Transfer to wire rack to cool.

**Batter can be refrigerated overnight and then baked in the morning.

Biscuits and Sausage Gravy

Fluffy biscuits and creamy sausage gravy is the stuff breakfast dreams are made of.

1 pound turkey sausage (Recipe pg. 10)

⅓ cup all-purpose flour

3-4 cups whole milk

½ teaspoon salt

2 teaspoons freshly ground black pepper

Fluffy Buttermilk Biscuits (Recipe pg. 41)

In a large skillet over medium heat, brown the sausage, breaking it into small pieces with a spatula. Sprinkle flour over sausage and stir to coat. Cook, stirring constantly for 2-3 minutes before slowly adding 3 cups of the milk. Continue cooking, stirring frequently until gravy has thickened. Season to taste with salt and pepper. Add more milk as needed if gravy gets too thick.

Serve immediately over warm biscuits.

"I come from a home where gravy is a beverage."
-Erma Bombeck

Homemade Turkey Sausage

Don't be intimidated by the number of ingredients in this recipe, it comes together with very little effort at all! Feel free to adjust seasoning to fit your own preferences. Liquid smoke can be omitted if desired, the sausage still packs a lot of flavor without it. For best flavor, refrigerate the sausage for a few hours or overnight.

1 pound ground turkey

½ teaspoon sea salt

1 teaspoon rubbed sage

1 teaspoon dried thyme

1 teaspoon freshly ground black pepper

¼ teaspoon cayenne

½ teaspoon garlic powder

Pinch of cloves

Pinch of nutmeg

Pinch of allspice

1 tablespoon pure maple syrup

¼ teaspoon hickory-flavored liquid smoke*

1 tablespoon olive oil (if shaping into patties)

In a medium bowl, mix all herbs and spices together. Add turkey to the bowl and mix well by hand. Add maple syrup, liquid smoke, and olive oil (if using). Mix until thoroughly combined. Cover and refrigerate for a few hours or overnight to allow the flavors to meld.

See pg. 248 for ingredient sources.

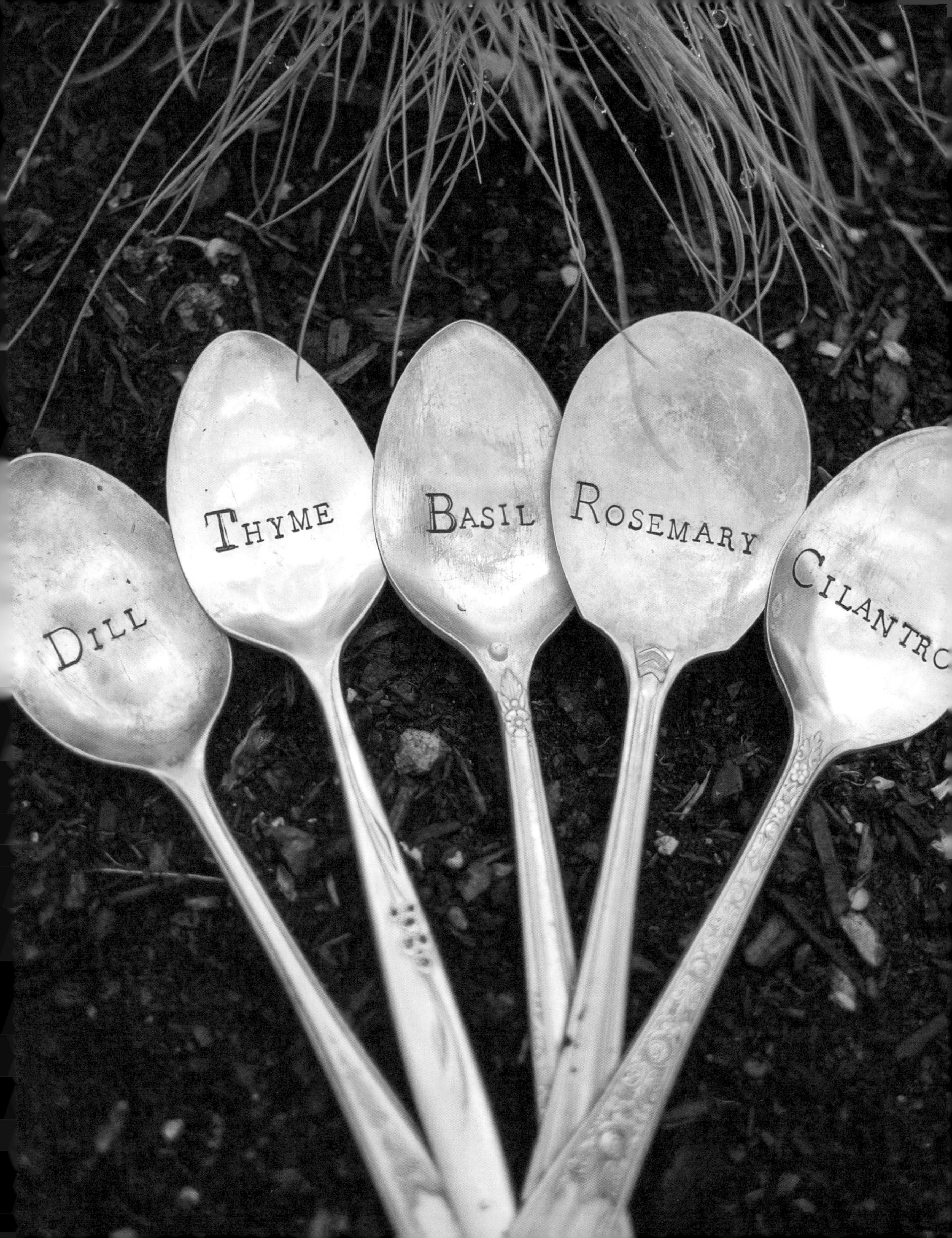
Dill
Thyme
Basil
Rosemary
Cilantro

Hot Cross Buns

Hot Cross Buns are a Good Friday tradition dating back to the days of Queen Elizabeth the First, and probably even earlier. It is my understanding that at that time, the sale of Hot Cross Buns was forbidden unless it was Good Friday or Christmas. Those caught disobeying the order would be forced to forfeit the contraband buns and give them to the poor. This prompted people to begin making them at home instead of purchasing them.

Truthfully, until about five years ago, the thought of hot cross buns typically triggered a flashback to 4th grade music class when we had to play the song on our recorders over and over and over. I'm pretty sure that was the origin of the "earworm"...

When it comes to making homemade Hot Cross Buns, there are a few different accepted techniques/variations which are largely a personal-preference issue it seems. Understandably so, people seem to think the version that their mothers and grandmothers made them every Easter season is the one and only right way to make them. Some use currants, some raisins, some a combination. Some make the cross by scoring the dough with a knife, some use icing to make the cross, and others use a flour mixture to make the cross. Egg wash, no egg wash. Sugar glaze, no glaze. The possibilities are endless. Go with your gut. If you like things heavier on spice, add a bit extra. I have no such pre-existing notions of the ideal Hot Cross Bun. I set out on my little Hot Cross Bun project with an open mind, and an arsenal of flour, spices, yeast, and raisins. Our favorite version uses a flour mixture to bake the cross shape on the top, and then is glazed with a sugar syrup immediately after baking, giving each bun an irresistibly glossy, sweet exterior to these perfectly spiced yeast rolls.

For the Dough-

3 ¼ cups unbleached bread flour, plus more as needed

2 ¼ teaspoons (1 envelope) active dry yeast

¼ cup granulated sugar

1 teaspoon salt

1 cup whole milk

¼ cup unsalted butter

1 egg

2 teaspoons cinnamon

½ teaspoon nutmeg

½ teaspoon allspice

½ teaspoon cloves

1 cup raisins

¼ cup all-purpose flour

2 tablespoons cold water

For the Glaze-

2 tablespoons granulated sugar

2 tablespoons boiling water

(Continued on following page...)

In a large bowl of a stand mixer, whisk together the bread flour, yeast, sugar, and salt.

In a small saucepan set over medium-low heat, heat the butter and milk together until the butter has melted and the milk is warm, about 100°F.

Make a well in the center of the dry ingredients and pour in the milk and butter mixture. Add the egg and stir together with a wooden spoon until the mixture comes together. Attach the dough hook to the mixer and knead until smooth and elastic, about 5 minutes, then knead by hand an additional minute or two. (If dough seems overly sticky, knead in additional bread flour one tablespoon at a time. Adding too much flour will result in a tough dough. You want the dough to be slightly sticky.)

Place the dough in a lightly oiled bowl and cover with plastic wrap and a tea towel. Allow the dough to rise in a warm place until doubled in size, about 1-2 hours.

Place raisins in a heatproof bowl and cover with boiling water. Let sit for 10 minutes. Drain and set aside.

Once dough has risen, remove from bowl and knead in the spices and raisins until evenly distributed. Divide dough into 12 equal portions and shape into buns. Place buns on a baking sheet lined with a silicone baking mat or parchment paper, leaving about 2 inches between each bun. (To Make Ahead: Cover and refrigerate the dough at this point, then remove from refrigerator about 2 ½ hours before you want to serve. Allow dough to come up to room temperature, about 1 hour, then continue with the recipe as follows...)

Cover the buns with plastic wrap and a tea towel and allow to rise again for an hour or two, until they have doubled in size.

Preheat oven to 425°F.

When the buns have risen, make a paste with the all-purpose flour and place in a piping bag (or a re-sealable plastic bag with the corner cut off). Pipe a cross onto each bun with the flour paste.

Bake the buns in the preheated oven until golden brown, about 15-20 minutes. When the buns are almost done baking, combine the sugar and boiling water to make the glaze.

Remove buns from oven and brush with sugar glaze immediately.

Note- Hot Cross Buns are best when enjoyed the same day they are baked, however they can be prepared the night before serving, if you wish. Simply prepare the recipe according to the directions up to the point when it is time for the second rise, then refrigerate. Remove from refrigerator in the morning, about 2 ½ hours before you would like to serve them, then allow dough to rise (second rising), and continue with the recipe directions.

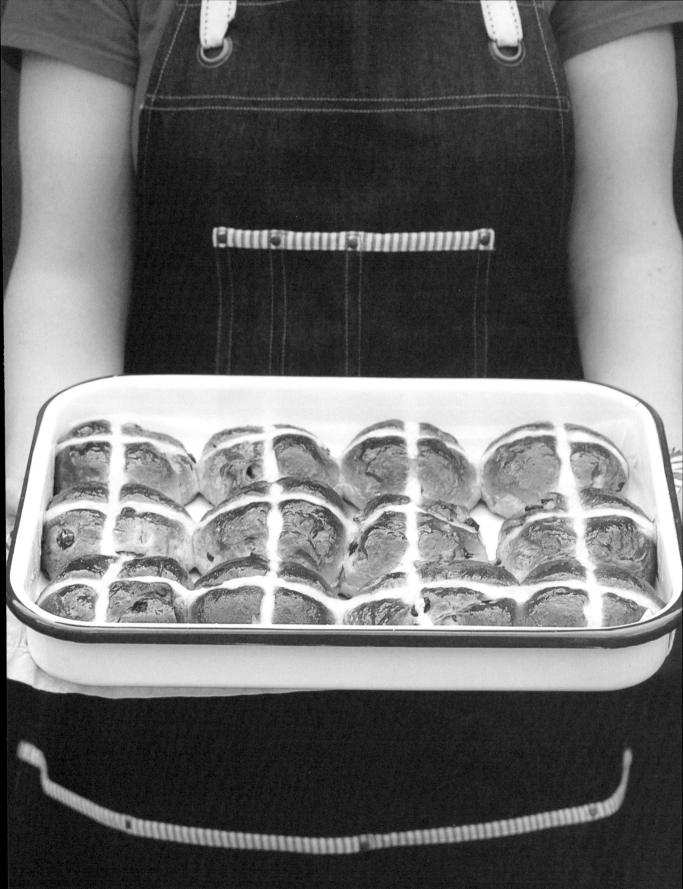

Bran Muffins

1 ½ cups wheat bran

1 cup sour cream

¼ cup milk

⅓ cup canola oil

1 egg

⅔ cup brown sugar

½ teaspoon pure vanilla extract

1 cup all-purpose flour

1 teaspoon baking soda

1 teaspoon baking powder

½ teaspoon salt

¾ cup dried cranberries, optional

Preheat oven to 375°F. Spray a muffin pan with cooking spray, or line with cupcake liners.

Place dried cranberries in a heatproof bowl and add enough boiling water to cover them completely. Let sit 10 minutes. Drain and set aside.

In a large bowl, combine wheat bran, sour cream, and milk. Stir until combined. Let sit 10 minutes.

In a medium bowl, whisk together oil, egg, brown sugar, and vanilla. Add to bowl with bran mixture and stir to combine.

In a separate bowl, whisk together the flour, baking soda, baking powder, and salt. Fold into wet ingredients.

Fold in cranberries, if using.

Divide batter into prepared muffin pan, filling each cup about ⅔ full.

Bake at 375°F for 15-20 minutes, or until toothpick comes out clean.

Let cool in pan for 5 minutes, then transfer muffins to a wire rack to cool completely.

Serve warm with butter.

Grand Haven, Michigan

Sour Cream Waffles

Weekends are for waffles, and these are some of my favorite. The slightly tangy flavor that the sour cream provides is the perfect base for all the sweet toppings you could ever want. Fresh blueberries and Warm Vanilla Sauce is a favorite combo at our cabin on sleepy Saturday mornings.

2 ¼ cups all-purpose flour

3 teaspoons baking powder

¾ teaspoon baking soda

¾ teaspoon salt

¼ cup granulated sugar

1 stick unsalted butter, melted

3 large eggs

1 tablespoon pure vanilla extract

1 ½ cups sour cream

¼ cup + 2 tablespoons whole milk

Fresh blueberries, for serving

Warm Vanilla Sauce (Recipe pg. 216)

Preheat waffle iron.

In a large bowl, whisk together the flour, baking powder, baking soda, salt, and sugar until combined. Set aside.

Preheat oven to 250°F.

In a medium bowl, combine melted butter, eggs, vanilla, sour cream, and milk until smooth. Pour into flour mixture and stir until just combined. Batter may be lumpy.

Spray preheated waffle iron with cooking spray and ladle batter onto waffles iron, cooking until golden.

Transfer cooked waffles to a baking sheet and place in oven to keep warm.

Repeat with remaining batter.

Serve warm, topped with fresh fruit, maple syrup, or Warm Vanilla Sauce if desired.

"Waffles are just awesome bread."
-John Green

Blueberry Dutch Baby

This giant, puffy, baked pancake has a delicate and subtle flavor that can be dressed up with any toppings or mix-ins that you might desire. Fresh berries, especially right after a trip to the orchard for a fun morning of blueberry picking. Since the batter itself isn't overly sweet, the dusting of powdered sugar or a drizzle of maple syrup really tops it off beautifully. If making the Dutch Baby plain, without any fruit mixed in, I highly recommend adding a little butter and a generous sprinkling of cinnamon and sugar to the top fresh out of the oven. This recipe is fun for the kids to watch through the oven door too. It "grows" very tall in the oven before deflating as it cools. Have fun!

3 large eggs

½ cup all-purpose flour

½ cup whole milk

1 tablespoon granulated sugar

½ teaspoon pure vanilla extract

Pinch cinnamon

4 tablespoons unsalted butter

¾ cup fresh blueberries

Confectioners' sugar, for dusting

Maple syrup for serving, if desired

Preheat oven to 425°F.

In a food processor or blender, add eggs, flour, milk, sugar, vanilla, and cinnamon. Blend until very smooth.

Place butter in a 10-inch cast iron skillet and set in preheated oven just until butter is melted, about 3 minutes.

Pour batter into hot skillet and top with blueberries.

Bake at 425°F for 17 minutes, then lower heat to 300°F and bake 5 minutes more.

Serve immediately.

Monkey Bread

Step away from the refrigerated biscuits in a tube. We're kicking things up a notch.

3 cups all-purpose flour

4 teaspoons baking powder

1 teaspoon salt

½ teaspoon cinnamon

⅓ cup unsalted butter, cubed and chilled

1 ¼ cups milk

¾ cup granulated sugar

¾ cup brown sugar (light or dark)

1 ½ teaspoons cinnamon

½ cup (1 stick) unsalted butter, melted

Preheat oven to 375°F. Generously spray a Bundt pan with cooking spray.

In a large bowl, whisk together the flour, baking powder, salt, and cinnamon.

Cut in cubed butter using a pastry blender or a fork until the butter is the size of small peas.

Pour in milk and stir until combined. Transfer dough to a floured surface and knead for a few seconds to bring dough together.

Add the melted butter to a small bowl. In a separate bowl, combine the granulated sugar, brown sugar, and cinnamon.

Shape the dough into balls just smaller than the size of a golf ball. Dip each ball of dough into the melted butter, then roll into the cinnamon-sugar mixture and arrange in the prepared pan. Repeat until no dough remains. Set aside any leftover butter and cinnamon-sugar mixture.

Bake at 375°F for 20-25 minutes until a toothpick inserted into the biscuits comes out clean. Let cool in the pan for 10 minutes, then gently loosen the monkey bread from the sides of the pan with a knife before turning out onto a serving plate.

Combine the leftover butter and cinnamon-sugar mixture in a small saucepan. Bring to a simmer over medium heat, stirring almost constantly until all sugar is dissolved. Drizzle over monkey bread and serve immediately.

Deep Dish Quiche

1 recipe pie crust, sugar omitted (Recipe pg. 228)

1 egg white (save yolk for filling)

8 slices thick-cut bacon, cut into small pieces

1 large onion, chopped fine, about 2 cups

1 ½ tablespoons cornstarch

3 cups half and half

8 large eggs plus 1 large yolk

½ teaspoon salt

¼ teaspoon pepper

Pinch nutmeg

Pinch cayenne pepper

1½ cups shredded Gruyere cheese

Preheat oven to 375°F with the rack set in the lower-middle position. Using a 9-inch Springform pan, blind bake the crust according to the method on pg. 228.

Remove crust from oven and brush immediately with egg white. Set aside while you prepare the filling. The egg white acts as a moisture barrier to prevent the crust from getting soggy.

Reduce oven temperature to 350°F.

Cook bacon in a skillet set over medium heat until crisp. Transfer to a paper towel-lined plate and set aside. Discard all but 2 tablespoons of fat from the pan. Return to medium heat and add chopped onion. Cook, stirring frequently, until softened and browned slightly, about 10 minutes. Set aside and allow to cool a bit.

In a large bowl, whisk together the cornstarch and 3 tablespoons of the half and half. Whisk in the remaining half and half, eggs, yolk, salt, pepper, nutmeg, and cayenne. Whisk until smooth.

Sprinkle the cheese, onions, and bacon in the bottom of the crust. Gently pour the egg mixture over the top.

Bake until top of quiche is golden and a toothpick inserted in the center comes out clean, 80-90 minutes. Transfer to a wire rack to cool at least 30 minutes. (Do not serve immediately after baking as the quiche needs time to cool and set or your slices won't come out clean.)

Note- Re-heating instructions: For best results, reheat in a 350°F oven for 10-15 minutes or until warmed through.

**This recipe will not fit in a standard pie plate.*

Pumpkin Donuts

One of the surest signals that Fall is coming to Michigan is when all of the apple orchards, cider mills, and pumpkin patches open up for the season. Weekend mornings bring folks out in droves to line up and wait for the fresh baked donuts at the local orchards. It's a rite of passage that must be experienced as often as possible while the leaves are golden and the air is crisp. Fortunately, making pumpkin donuts at home is not as difficult as it may sound, and can be enjoyed no matter the location or season.

For the Donuts-

3 ½ cups all purpose flour
4 teaspoons baking powder
1 teaspoon salt
1 teaspoon ground cinnamon
½ teaspoon ground ginger
½ teaspoon baking soda
¼ teaspoon ground nutmeg
⅛ teaspoon ground cloves
1 cup sugar
3 tablespoons unsalted butter, room temperature
1 large egg
2 large egg yolks
1 teaspoon vanilla extract
½ cup plus 1 tablespoon buttermilk
1 cup canned pure pumpkin
Canola oil (for deep-frying)

For the Spiced Sugar-

1 cup sugar
4 teaspoons ground cinnamon
2 teaspoons ground nutmeg

For the Glaze-

1 ½ cups confectioners' sugar
2 tablespoons melted butter
2 tablespoons whole milk
1 teaspoon pure vanilla extract
pinch cinnamon
pinch nutmeg
pinch cloves

For Spiced Sugar-

Whisk sugar, cinnamon, and nutmeg in a bowl until combined. Set aside.

For Donuts-

Whisk together the flour, baking powder, salt, cinnamon, ginger, baking soda, nutmeg, and cloves until combined.

In the bowl of a stand mixer fitted with the paddle attachment, mix sugar and butter together on medium speed until blended. Reduce speed to low, then add egg, then yolks and vanilla. Gradually mix in buttermilk, then add pumpkin in 4 additions.

Using rubber spatula, fold in dry ingredients in 4 additions, blending gently after each addition. Cover with plastic; chill 3 hours.

(Continued on following page...)

Pumpkin Donuts, Cont.

Sprinkle 2 rimmed baking sheets lightly with flour. Press out ⅓ of dough on floured surface to ½- to ⅔-inch thickness. Using a 2½-inch-diameter round cutter, cut out dough rounds. Arrange on sheets.

Repeat with remaining dough in 2 more batches. Gather dough scraps. Press out dough and cut out more dough rounds until all dough is used.

Using 1-inch-diameter round cutter, cut out center of each dough round to make doughnuts and doughnut holes.

Line 2 baking sheets with several layers of paper towels. Pour oil into large deep skillet to depth of 1½ inches. Attach deep-fry thermometer and heat oil to 365°F to 370°F.

Fry donut holes in 2 batches until golden brown, turning occasionally, about 2 minutes. Using slotted spoon, transfer to paper towels to drain.

Fry donuts, 3 or 4 at a time, until golden brown, adjusting heat to maintain temperature, about 1 minute per side. Using slotted spoon, transfer doughnuts to paper towels to drain. Allow to drain on paper towel for about 1 minute, then glaze or roll in spiced sugar.

For the Glaze-
In a small bowl, whisk together the confectioners' sugar, melted butter, milk, vanilla, cinnamon, nutmeg, and cloves until very smooth. Dip donuts into glaze, or drizzle glaze over the top of the donuts.

Serve with warm apple cider. Best enjoyed while wearing plaid.

Breakfast Burritos

1 tablespoon oil

½ pound ground sausage

1 pound shredded hash brown potatoes

1 green pepper, seeded and chopped

1 medium onion, chopped

6 large eggs, lightly beaten

½ teaspoon salt

¼ teaspoon pepper

Flour tortillas (Recipe pg. 57)

8 ounces sharp cheddar cheese, shredded

½ cup mayonnaise

1 tablespoon hot sauce, plus more to taste

Sour cream, for serving

Hot sauce, for serving

Prepare the spicy cream sauce by whisking together ½ cup mayonnaise with 1 tablespoon hot sauce. Add more hot sauce if desired. Set aside to allow flavors to meld.

In a large skillet, heat 1 tablespoon oil over medium-high heat. Cook sausage until browned, breaking it into bite-sized pieces with spatula while cooking.

Transfer sausage to a paper-towel lined plate to drain. Set aside.

Reserve 2 tablespoons of fat from the sausage in the skillet. Add potatoes, onion, and green pepper to skillet and cook over medium-high heat until cooked through and the potatoes are golden.

Return sausage to pan. Add eggs, salt, and pepper. Cook, stirring frequently with spatula until eggs have cooked through. Adjust seasoning to taste

Warm tortillas in microwave or skillet. Top each tortilla with about ¾ cup of the filling and sprinkle with cheese. Roll tortillas and drizzle with sauce.

Serve immediately with sour cream and hot sauce, if desired.

Bacon and Sweet Corn Breakfast Galette

There are very few things that can compete with fresh Michigan sweet corn in the Summer. I would eat it at every meal if possible during the harvest season. For best results, use fresh corn from the cob in this recipe. Omitting the corn if it is not in season is an option, but do not substitute with canned or frozen corn if at all possible.. Trust me. it's not the same recipe without using the real thing.

Half-batch Hot Water Crust, chilled (Recipe pg. 229)

2 pounds red potatoes, cleaned and cubed (about 8 medium sized potatoes)

1 pound bacon, cut into 1-inch pieces

2 ears fresh sweet corn, cut from cob

1 medium onion, chopped

3 green onions, sliced thin

6 cooked eggs with runny yolks

Salt and pepper, to taste

1 large egg + 1 tablespoon water, lightly beaten

Preheat oven to 375°F. Line a baking sheet with parchment paper.

In a large skillet over medium heat, cook the bacon. Remove to a paper towel lined plate.

Add potatoes and onion, cooking until potatoes are just starting to brown, but not quite tender. Turn off heat. Return bacon to pan. Stir in corn kernels. Season with salt and pepper to taste.

On a floured surface, roll out chilled dough into a large circle, about 18-inches in diameter. Transfer to parchment-lined baking sheet. Add filling to center of dough, leaving about 3-inches on all sides. Fold dough over the edge of the filling in 6 sections, leaving center of filling exposed. Brush dough with egg wash and sprinkle with salt and pepper.

Bake at 375°F 30-35 minutes, or until crust is golden brown. In the last several minutes of baking time, cook the eggs.

Slice into wedges and top with runny egg. The yolk will act as a sauce.

Serve immediately.

Malted Pancakes

Although subtle, the malted milk powder adds a layer of flavor to liven up these pancakes. Serve with butter and syrup, or get a bit more creative and top with Caramel-Banana Syrup (Recipe pg. 223)

2 eggs

1 cup plus 2 tablespoons buttermilk

3 tablespoons canola oil

1 ½ cups all-purpose flour

¼ cup malted milk powder

¾ teaspoon kosher salt

1 ½ teaspoons baking powder

¼ teaspoon baking soda

1 teaspoon pure vanilla extract

In a large bowl, beat eggs and buttermilk together with an electric mixer until foamy. Add oil and vanilla and mix until combined.

In a medium bowl, whisk together the flour, malted milk powder, salt, baking powder, and baking soda until combined.

Add flour mixture to egg mixture and mix gently just until combined.

Let batter rest for 15 minutes.

Heat a nonstick skillet to 375°F.

Spray skillet with nonstick spray, then add batter to pan, using ¼ cup per pancake.

Cook for 2 minutes, flip, then cook another 1 ½ minutes. Repeat with remaining batter.

Makes about 12 pancakes.

Serve immediately with pure maple syrup, or desired sauces. (See pgs. 216, 223 for homemade syrups and sauces.)

Note: This batter also works well when made into waffles.

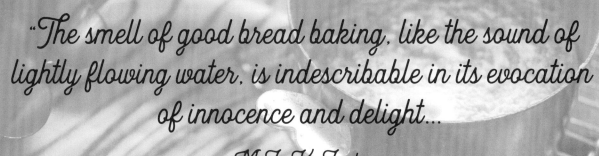

"The smell of good bread baking, like the sound of lightly flowing water, is indescribable in its evocation of innocence and delight...

-M.F.K. Fisher

Breads, Biscuits, & Rolls

Fluffy Buttermilk Biscuits

Make good choices. Bake great biscuits.

2 cups self-rising flour

¼ cup lard, chilled

1 cup cold buttermilk

Butter, for baking sheet

Preheat oven to 450°F. Spread baking sheet with butter.

In a medium bowl, cut flour into lard with a fork or pastry cutter until mixture resembles coarse crumbs. Pour buttermilk into flour mixture and stir just until combined.

Turn dough out onto a lightly floured surface and roll into a rectangle, about ½-inch thick. Fold dough over itself, then roll out again. Repeat folding and rolling, leaving the dough ¾-1 inch thick. Cut into rounds using a floured biscuit cutter or the rim of a glass.

Arrange biscuits onto prepared baking sheet so that they're just touching each other.

Bake on center rack 11-13 minutes until golden.

Serve warm with Cinnamon-Honey Butter (Recipe pg. 225), jam, or with Sausage Gravy (Recipe pg. 8)

Makes about one dozen biscuits.

What could be more important than a little something to eat?
–Winnie the Pooh

Honey Wheat Sandwich Bread

This is my very favorite homemade bread recipe. I've made it for years and I never tire of it. A loaf fresh from the oven tastes like home and smells like heaven.

3 cups warm water

4 ½ teaspoons (2 envelopes) active dry yeast

⅔ cup honey, divided

5 cups bread flour

3 tablespoons melted butter

1 tablespoon salt

3 cups whole wheat flour, plus more as needed

1 additional tablespoons melted butter, for brushing crust

Make the Sponge: Combine warm water, yeast, and ⅓ cup honey in a very large bowl. Stir in bread flour. Cover with plastic wrap and let rise 30 minutes until risen and bubbly.

In a small bowl, mix together the melted butter, remaining ⅓ cup honey, and salt. Stir into the sponge. Stir in 2 cups of whole wheat flour. Knead in just enough of the remaining cup of flour that the dough is smooth and tacky, but not overly sticky. Let rise in greased bowl until doubled, about 1 hour.

Once risen, punch down dough and divide into 2 loaves. Place each loaf into a greased 9x5-inch loaf pan. Let rise until dough has risen 1-inch above the rim of the pans. Cut a slit into the top of the dough if you would like a split-top loaf.

Preheat oven to 350°F.

Bake 25-30 minutes, or until golden brown. Remove loaves from oven and brush tops immediately with melted butter. This step allows the top crust to stay nice and soft.

Let cool in pans 10 minutes before removing to a wire rack to cool completely before storing.

Makes two loaves.

Soft Pretzels & Pretzel Buns

Homemade pretzels don't have to be intimidating. Just go for it and make soft pretzels that are even better than at the mall. Serve with homemade hot cherry mustard, or roll in cinnamon and sugar and dip in warm Nutella sauce to make a dessert of them. Otherwise, if shaping the dough into pretzels makes you nervous, just start with pretzel buns. They're fantastic for sliders. You really can't go wrong.

2 ¼ teaspoons (1 envelope) instant yeast

1 ½ cups warm water (around 105°F)

1 teaspoon salt

1 tablespoon brown sugar

2 tablespoons melted butter

4 cups all-purpose flour

1 large egg

1 tablespoon cold water

9 cups water

½ cup baking soda

Coarse sea salt for topping, optional

Hot Cherry Mustard, for serving (Recipe pg. 210)

In a large bowl, whisk together the yeast and warm water. Let sit 1 minute, then add salt, sugar, and butter and whisk until combined. Gradually add flour and stir until combined.

Using floured hands and a lightly floured surface, knead dough for about 3 minutes until dough is smooth and bounces back slightly when pressed. Cover and let rest in an oiled bowl for 30 minutes.

While dough is resting, prepare the baking soda bath. In a large pot over high heat, combine water and baking soda, stirring until dissolved. Once mixture comes to a boil, reduce heat to medium-low and continue to boil gently.

Preheat oven to 425°F. Line two rimmed baking sheets with parchment paper or silpat baking liners.

Divide dough into 4 portions. Using one portion at a time, roll dough into a long rope and cut into 8-inch lengths. Shape into pretzels (see pg. 46) and arrange on prepared baking sheets. Repeat with remaining dough. (For pretzel buns, shape dough into balls about 2 to 3-inches in diameter.)

Drop 3 or 4 pretzels at a time into the baking soda bath for 30 seconds. Remove with a fine mesh sieve and drain off any excess liquid. Return pretzels to baking sheet.

Repeat with remaining pretzels, adjusting heat as needed to maintain a gentle boil.

In a small bowl, whisk together the egg and 1 tablespoon of water.

Brush pretzels with egg wash, then bake at 425°F for 12-14 minutes until golden.

Top with coarse salt.

-HOW TO SHAPE A PRETZEL-

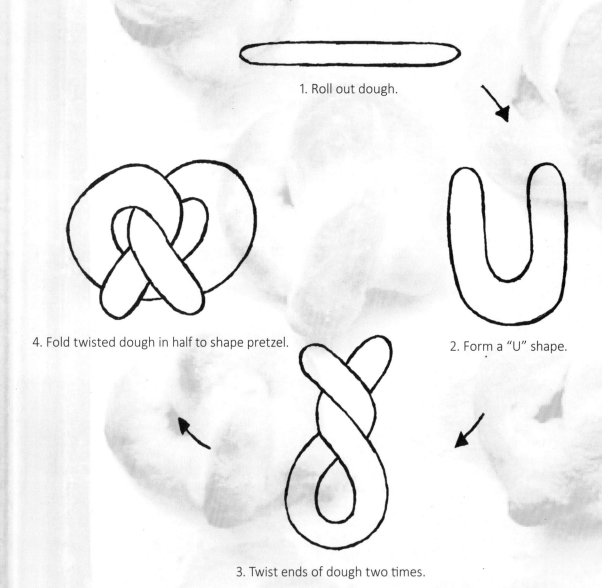

1. Roll out dough.

2. Form a "U" shape.

3. Twist ends of dough two times.

4. Fold twisted dough in half to shape pretzel.

Cinnamon-Sugar Soft Pretzels

¼ cup melted butter

¾ cup granulated sugar

2 ½ teaspoons cinnamon

Melt the ¼ cup of butter in a small bowl. Combine cinnamon and sugar in another small bowl.

Follow recipe for Soft Pretzels (pg. 45). Instead of topping the finished pretzels with coarse salt, dip baked pretzels into the melted butter, letting excess butter drip off, then roll in cinnamon-sugar mixture.

Return to baking sheet. Continue with remaining pretzels.

Serve with Warm Nutella Sauce, (Recipe pg. 216)

**Note:* For best results, dip pretzels in butter and cinnamon-sugar the same day you plan to enjoy them. If you would like to save some for another day, store baked uncoated pretzels in an airtight container. Warm the pretzels in the oven for a few minutes and then proceed with the butter and cinnamon-sugar coating the day you'll be enjoying them. The coated pretzels do not keep well overnight because the sugar dissolves and turns very messy.

These pretzels are making me thirsty.
-Cosmo Kramer

When I think of beer bread, I typically envision quick bread baked in a loaf pan. This is not that kind of beer bread. This is a flavorful yeast bread that is amazing with a pat of butter served alongside a hearty supper, or sliced for a chicken salad sandwich on a random Tuesday, or my personal favorite- epic French Toast. Just trust me on this one. You'll keep a bottle of beer in the pantry just for making this bread when the mood strikes.

Yeasted Beer Bread

1 cup beer*

⅓ cup water

2 tablespoons canola oil

3 ½ cups bread flour, divided

3 tablespoons sugar

½ teaspoon salt

1 ½ teaspoons Red Star Platinum instant yeast

Cooking spray

Cornmeal for sprinkling

In a small saucepan, heat the beer, water, and oil to 120-130°F

In the large bowl of a stand mixer fitted with the paddle attachment, combine 1 cup bread flour, sugar, salt, and yeast. Add beer mixture and mix on low until combined, scraping down bowl as needed. Increase speed to medium and beat for 4 minutes. Scrape down bowl again. Add remaining 2 ½ cups bread flour and switch to dough hook. Knead on medium speed for 6 minutes. Dough should be firm yet smooth and elastic but not overly sticky. Use additional flour if needed.

Transfer dough to a greased bowl and turn to coat. Cover with plastic wrap and let rest at room temperature until until nearly doubled in bulk and when pressed with two fingers, it leaves an impression. Transfer dough to a lightly floured surface and punch down to remove air bubbles. Shape dough into 12-18-inch rectangle. Starting with the short side, tightly roll up dough and pinch the edges to seal. Pinch ends and tuck seams underneath the loaf.

Spray a rimmed baking sheet with cooking spray and sprinkle lightly with cornmeal. Place shaped loaf onto prepared baking sheet. Using a very sharp knife or a straight razor, slash the top of the dough 4 times. Cover with plastic wrap and let rest again, about 45 minutes, until dough slowly springs back when gently pressed with 1 finger..

Preheat oven to 375°F. Bake 30-40 minutes until golden and sounds hollow when tapped.

Transfer to wire rack to cool completely before slicing.

For best flavor, use a beer that is not hoppy. Oatmeal stouts are excellent in this recipe, such as New Holland Brewing's The Poet. Roak Brewing Company's French Toast Oatmeal Stout is also fantastic because it is brewed with maple syrup.

Potato Rolls

The best rolls ever. Serve with Cinnamon Honey Butter (Recipe pg.225) and your life will never be the same. They're also fantastic sandwich rolls for Thanksgiving leftovers.

3 cups whole milk

1 cup (2 sticks) unsalted butter, softened

¾ cup granulated sugar

2 large russet potatoes

1 tablespoon salt

2 ¼ teaspoons (1 envelope) instant yeast

4 large eggs, lightly beaten

8 cups all-purpose flour, divided

Preheat oven to 400°F.

Bake the potatoes on a large rimmed baking sheet for 60 minutes until very soft.. Let sit a few minutes until cool enough to handle. Cut potatoes in half lengthwise and remove as much flesh from the skins as needed to yield 1 cup. Mash in a bowl with a fork to remove any lumps. Set aside.

Line two rimmed baking sheets with parchment paper. Spray lightly with cooking spray.

Add 7 cups flour to a large mixing bowl. Set aside remaining cup of flour to use when rolling out dough.

In a medium saucepan, scald the milk by heating it over medium heat until foam forms around the edges but milk does not reach a boil.

Turn off heat and add ¾ cup (1 ½ sticks) butter, sugar, potatoes, and salt. Stir to combine and let cool until lukewarm. (Set aside remaining ¼ cup butter to get very soft for use when rolling out dough.)

Add yeast, then eggs and stir until thoroughly combined. Add milk mixture to the flour mixture and stir until all flour has incorporated. Dough will be very sticky.

Cover with plastic wrap and let rise at room temperature for 1 hour.

With floured hands, punch down dough. (The messy hands will be worth it. Trust me on this one.)

On a very well-floured surface, roll out one-third of the dough into a large rectangle, sprinkling with additional flour as needed. Spread one half of the rectangle with one-third of the softened butter.

Fold dough over the buttered portion and press edges lightly to seal. Roll out again to form a rectangle. Cut dough into 8 triangles and roll dough up starting from the wide end of the triangle.

Arrange on prepared baking sheets. Repeat with remaining dough.

Cover rolls with plastic wrap and let rise until nearly doubled in size, about 2 hours at room temperature.

Preheat oven to 350°F.

Bake 13-16 minutes, until golden. Let cool slightly before removing from baking sheets to serve.

Cinnamon Swirl Quick Bread

4 cups all-purpose flour

2 teaspoons baking soda

¼ teaspoon salt

1 cup unsalted butter, softened

2 cups granulated sugar

2 eggs

2 cups buttermilk

1 teaspoon pure vanilla extract

⅔ cups additional granulated sugar

2 teaspoons cinnamon

Preheat oven to 350°F. Spray 2 loaf pans with nonstick spray.

Whisk flour, baking soda, and salt together in a large bowl.

In the bowl of a stand mixer fitted with the paddle attachment, beat the butter and sugar together until completely incorporated. Add eggs and vanilla and continue mixing. With the mixer on low speed, add ½ of the flour mixture, followed by the buttermilk, then the remaining flour mixture. Mix until just combined.

Spread ¼ of the batter into the bottom of each loaf pan, using half the batter.

Mix together the sugar and cinnamon and sprinkle ⅔ of the mixture over the batter in each of the pans.

Spread the remaining batter into the loaf pans and top with remaining cinnamon sugar mixture. Using a knife or toothpick, make a few swirls in the batter.

Bake at 350°F for 50-60 minutes or until a toothpick comes out clean when inserted.

Cool loaves in pans for 20 minutes before removing from pan and slicing.

Oatmeal Bread

6 cups bread flour

2 cups rolled oats, plus 2 tablespoons for sprinkling

4 tablespoons unsalted butter, at room temperature

1 tablespoon salt

6 tablespoons dark brown sugar

2 envelopes (4 ½ teaspoons) instant yeast

2 ½ cups whole milk, lukewarm (around 105°F)

Combine all ingredients in the bowl of a stand mixer fitted with the dough hook. Turn mixer to medium speed and knead 10 minutes with dough hook.

Transfer dough to a greased bowl. Cover with plastic wrap and a tea towel, then let rise for 1 hour.

Punch down dough, divide in two, and shape into loaves. Arrange shaped dough into loaf pans sprayed with cooking spray.

Cover and let rise for 1½ hours. Sprinkle with remaining oats and gently press them into the dough to keep them in place.

Bake at 350°F for 35 to 40 minutes.until golden brown and bread sounds hollow when tapped.

Make 2 loaves.

Flour Tortillas

We go through tortillas at an incredible pace in our house. They're so versatile and can be used for quick sandwiches on-the-go, breakfast burritos, salsa verde chicken enchiladas for dinner, or Taco Tuesday, of course.

4 cups all-purpose flour

1 teaspoon sea salt

2 teaspoons baking powder

2 tablespoons lard

1 ½ cups water

In a large bowl, combine flour, salt, baking powder, and lard. Using a pastry cutter, fork, or clean fingers, work the lard into the dry ingredients until the texture resembles cornmeal.

Gradually add water until dough comes together.

Divide dough into 24 balls.

Using a floured surface and a rolling pin, roll each ball of dough until thin. Each tortilla should measure about 8-inches in diameter. Repeat with remaining dough.

In a large dry nonstick skillet over medium-high heat, cook tortillas until bubbled up and golden, then flip and cook other side until golden.

Repeat with remaining dough.

To keep tortillas from drying out, seal them in an airtight zipper storage bag while they are still warm. Keep refrigerated for up to two weeks. Warm before serving.

"Pull up a chair. Take a taste. Come join us.
Life is so endlessly delicious."

–Ruth Reichl

Soups, Salads, & Sandwiches

Brussels Sprout and Bacon Salad
with Pears and Maple Vinaigrette

Looking for a salad that will stand out from the crowd at your next holiday gathering? Give this Winter salad a try. Tart cranberries, smoky, salty bacon, and a tangy yet sweet Maple Syrup Vinagrette is sure to please even those who think they don't like brussels sprouts.

¾ pound brussels sprouts, shaved

¼ pound Applewood smoked bacon, cooked and roughly chopped

1 fresh pear, sliced thin

⅓ cup dried cranberries

¼ cup toasted pecans

Maple Syrup Vinaigrette (Recipe pg. 206)

Toss brussels sprouts with maple vinaigrette in a large bowl. Divide into serving dishes. Arrange bacon, pear slices, cranberries, and toasted pecans on top of Brussels sprouts. Serve with additional dressing on the side.

Caprese Salad

While living in Italy, I rode my bicycle, "Bluebell" (she was blue and had a bell...) all around our little town gathering the ingredients I would need for the next day or so and filling my little basket. The furthest stop on my route was the cheese shop for mozzarella di bufalo. A worthwhile trip. Fresh mozzazrella made from buffalo milk. It was tangy and fabulous. I got to watch the gentlemen making it daily and given the opportunity, I would have loved to spend my days there learning the craft. I settled for eating it on a daily basis, so I'm not complaining. When purchasing fresh mozzarella in the U.S., a good rule of thumb is to buy the balls of mozzarella that are packed in liquid instead of vacuum packed.

2 (8-ounce) balls fresh mozzarella (buffalo mozzarella, if you can find it)

2-3 ripe tomatoes

Fresh basil leaves

Drizzle of extra-virgin olive oil

Drizzle of Balsamic Glaze (Recipe pg. 207)

Coarse sea salt

Arrange mozzarella, tomatoes, and basil as you would like. Slicing and layering the tomatoes and mozzarella make it pretty, but also makes it easy to get even amounts of each ingredient in every bite.

Drizzle with olive oil and balsamic glaze. Season with coarse sea salt to taste.

Green Salad with Grilled Chicken, Apples, and Cranberries

Fresh spring mix salad greens, torn

2 boneless skinless chicken breasts, grilled, cooled, and sliced

1 Granny Smith or other tart apple, cut into bite-size pieces

½ cup dried cranberries

Salt and pepper to taste

Apple Cider Vinaigrette (Recipe pg. 206)

Arrange all ingredients in a large bowl. Toss with dressing. Serve immediately.

Elaine: Can I have a big salad?

Waitress: A big salad?

Elaine: You see...

George: Just tell them what you want. They'll make it for you.

Elaine: It's a salad, only bigger, with lots of stuff in it.

Waitress: I can bring you two small salads.

Elaine: Could you put it in a big bowl?

Waitress: We don't have big bowls.

Elaine: All right, just get me a cup of decaf.

-Seinfeld

Riviera Salad

This salad is my version of a wildly popular signature salad at a local family-owned bakery and cafe in the Grand Rapids area. Fresh fruit, toasted pecans, and a sweet-yet-tangy poppyseed vinaigrette make this salad my favorite warm weather salad for many reasons, but one of which is definitely the memories it brings back from the early days when I was pregnant with my oldest daughter and I craved these on a nearly daily basis. Feel free to substitute any available fresh fruit as desired.

Crisp romaine lettuce, roughly torn/chopped

Fresh strawberries, hulled and sliced

Fresh blueberries

1 cup chopped pecans

Riviera dressing (Recipe pg. 207)

Toast pecans in a dry skillet over medium heat until fragrant. Transfer to a bowl and let cool.

Toss lettuce, strawberries, blueberries, and pecans in a large salad bowl.

Drizzle Riviera dressing over the top and toss until salad greens are lightly coated.

Smoked Whitefish Chowder

1 ½ pounds Yukon gold potatoes, cut into chunks

1 cup heavy cream

1 cup milk

1 teaspoon salt

½ teaspoon freshly ground black pepper

1 tablespoon unsalted butter

1 tablespoon olive oil

1 medium onion, finely chopped

3 stalks celery, chopped fine

1 teaspoon chopped fresh thyme

1 cup dry white wine*

3 ½ cups low-sodium chicken stock

3 ears fresh sweet corn (shaved from cob)

2 pounds smoked whitefish, flaked with fork**

2 tablespoons chopped fresh dill

2 tablespoons chopped fresh parsley

Hot sauce, to taste

In a medium saucepan, combine potatoes, cream, milk, salt, and pepper. Bring to a boil then reduce to a simmer. Cook, stirring occasionally for 15 minutes, until potatoes are tender.

In a large pot or Dutch oven, heat butter and olive oil over medium heat. Add onion, celery, and thyme, cooking until softened.

Add wine to pot and boil until nearly evaporated, scraping the bottom of the pan with a wooden spatula. Add chicken stock. Taste and add salt as needed.

Transfer potatoes and cream mixture to the pot. Add corn kernels and simmer until tender.

Stir in flaked Whitefish, parsley, and dill. Add a few drops of hot sauce to taste.

Serve immediately.

*Michigan wine recommendations- Chateau Fontaine's Riesling or Chateau Chantal's Naughty White

**See pg. 248 for ingredient sources.

Michigan Cherry Chicken Salad

I could eat this chicken salad every single day and never tire of it. We love packing it in our picnic basket during the Summer when we go to the free outdoor concerts on Tuesday nights at our local botanical garden.

¾ cup dried Montmorency cherries (6 ounce bag)

1 cup boiling water

1 ¼ cups mayonnaise

½ cup chopped pecans

¼ cup finely diced celery

½ teaspoon salt

½ teaspoon freshly ground black pepper

4 cups cubed cooked chicken breast (about 2 breasts)

Place dried cherries in a small bowl and add just enough boiling water to cover. Let sit 5 minutes or until softened and plumped. Drain.

In a large bowl, combine mayonnaise, pecans, celery, salt, and pepper. Stir until combined. Add cherries and chicken, stirring until evenly distributed. Cover and refrigerate at least 4 hours before serving.

Garden Tomato Sandwiches

This non-recipe earns a place in this book by virtue of the fact that my daughter begs for a tomato sandwich every day of the Summer. She loves to go pick the tomatoes from our little backyard garden, and sometimes she even lets them get ripe first.

White sandwich bread

Mayonnaise

Sea salt

Freshly ground black pepper

Ripe garden tomatoes, any variety

Thinly slice tomatoes and sprinkle with salt and pepper.

Arrange two slices of bread on a plate.

Spread mayonnaise on both slices of bread. Arrange tomatoes on one slice of bread, season with additional salt and pepper, if desired. Top with remainig slice of bread.

Slice in half lengthwise, making two rectangles.

Serve and enjoy.

Repeat daily until no tomatoes remain in the garden.

*"It's difficult to think anything but pleasant thoughts
while eating a homegrown tomato."*

–Lewis Grizzard

Cucumber Sandwiches

This has been one of the most popular recipes on my website for years, and for good reason. It's such a simple, yet elegant offering for bridal showers, ladies' brunches, baby showers, or to accompany an afternoon tea. It's also a great way to enjoy fresh cucumbers from the garden for lunch on a run-of-the-mill weekday.

8 ounces cream cheese, softened

⅓ cup mayonnaise

¼ teaspoon salt

¼ teaspoon freshly ground black pepper

⅛ teaspoon garlic powder

2 tablespoons chopped fresh dill

1 ¼ cups peeled, seeded, diced cucumber

16 slices sandwich bread

In a medium bowl, beat cream cheese and mayonnaise with an electric mixer until smooth.

Add salt, pepper, garlic powder, and dill, mixing until combined.

Stir in diced cucumber.

Spread evenly on 8 slices of bread.

Top with remaining bread slices.

Using a serrated knife, remove crusts and cut each sandwich into four triangles.

Serve immediately.

Make-ahead: If desired, prepare the filling up to 2 days in advance and store in an airtight container in the refrigerator. Assemble sandwiches shortly before serving to prevent bread from getting soggy.

Roasted Butternut Squash Soup

This soup is Fall in a bowl. Serve with a salad for a nice lunch or light dinner. Also accompanies Maple Glazed Pork Loin very well. (Recipe pg. 111)

1 butternut squash, halved lengthwise and seeds removed

Olive oil

Salt and pepper, to taste

1 tablespoons olive oil

1 large sweet onion, finely chopped

1 Granny Smith apple, peeled, cored, and chopped fine

2 cloves garlic, minced

3 cups low sodium chicken stock

½ cup apple cider

1 ½ tablespoons pure maple syrup

1 teaspoon salt

Pinch ground nutmeg

Pinch ground sage

¼ cup heavy cream for drizzling

Preheat oven to 425°F.

Brush squash with olive oil and season with salt and pepper. Lay skin-side down on an oiled baking sheet. Place in oven and roast for 40 minutes, until cooked completely through and very tender.

Remove from oven and set aside. Once cool enough to handle, remove squash from the skin and transfer to a bowl.

In a Dutch oven or soup pot, heat oil over medium heat. Add onion and apple and sauté until onion is translucent and apple is tender. Add garlic and cook until fragrant, stirring constantly. Add reserved squash, chicken stock, apple cider, maple syrup, salt, nutmeg, and sage. Bring soup just to a boil then reduce heat to low to maintain a simmer.

Continue simmering for 20 minutes, stirring occasionally. Use an immersion blender or transfer soup to a blender in batches and blend until very smooth. Taste and season with salt and pepper as needed.

Serve hot and top with a drizzle of cream.

"One of the great gifts that you can give people is to cook for them."

–Ina Garten

Vegetables & Sides

Baked Sweet Potato Fries
with Maple Dipping Sauce

3 or 4 sweet potatoes, rinsed and peeled.

¼ cup cornstarch

¼ cup tapioca starch*

2 teaspoons salt

2 teaspoons smoked paprika

2 teaspoons garlic powder

1 teaspoon freshly ground black pepper

Pinch of cayenne

Pinch of ground cinnamon

4 tablespoons canola oil

Maple Dipping Sauce-

¼ cup mayonnaise

¼ cup pure maple syrup

Pinch of cayenne

Cut potatoes into matchsticks of desired thickness. Add potatoes to a large bowl of cold water and let soak for 30 minutes. Rinse and drain. Pat dry with paper towel.

Line two baking sheets with foil and spray with cooking spray. Preheat oven to 425°F.

Combine cornstarch and tapioca starch in a large zipper storage bag. Add potatoes and toss until coated evenly.

In a large mixing bowl, mix together the salt, paprika, garlic powder, black pepper, cayenne, and cinnamon. Add potatoes to bowl and drizzle with 2 tablespoons of the canola oil. Toss to coat, adding additional oil if needed to lightly coat all of the potatoes with the oil and seasonings.

Arrange potatoes in a single layer on prepared baking sheets.

Bake for 15 minutes, flip potatoes over, and bake 10-15 minutes more until tender and golden. Turn off oven, open door slightly, and let cool in oven for 10 minutes before serving.

Adjust seasoning to taste as needed.

While fries are cooling, mix mayonnaise and maple syrup in a small bowl until smooth.

Serve fries hot with dipping sauce.

See pg. 248 for ingredient sources.

Grilled Asparagus

If you haven't grilled asparagus before, you're missing out on the best way to enjoy asparagus, in my opinion. It's so simple to prepare, and cooks rather quickly, so you can arrange it on the grill with whatever else you're cooking and you've got a complete meal in no time.

1 bunch fresh asparagus spears, ends of stalks trimmed

2 tablespoons olive oil

Salt and pepper

Preheat a charcoal or gas grill to medium heat for direct cooking.

Toss asparagus with olive oil until lightly coated. Sprinkle with salt and pepper.

Arrange asparagus in an even layer on preheated grill.

Cook for about 8-12 minutes, turning asparagus as needed to ensure even cooking.

Test frequently for tenderness by poking stalks with the tip of a sharp knife.

Transfer to a serving platter and serve immediately.

Balsamic Glazed Carrots

2 pounds carrots, cleaned, peeled, cut into equal-size pieces

2 tablespoons unsalted butter

1 tablespoon granulated sugar

1 teaspoon salt

½ cup balsamic glaze (Recipe pg. 207)

In a medium saucepan, add the carrots, 1 tablespoon of butter, sugar, and salt. Add enough water to cover the carrots. Bring to a boil then lower heat to a simmer. Cook until carrots are tender and water has nearly evaporated, about 8-10 minutes.

To serve: Warm ½ cup of the Balsamic Glaze in a small saucepan and add remaining 1 tablespoon of butter, stirring until melted and combined.

Drizzle glaze over cooked carrots. Serve immediately with additional glaze on the side.

Grand Haven, Michigan

Jellied Cranberry Sauce

My husband is a hard core fan of cranberry sauce that is the shape of a can. It took me a while to come up with a homemade version that we both love, but now we will never buy it from the store again! This is a staple at our Thanksgiving table every year. It's also amazing on turkey sandwiches.

½ cup apple cider

1 cup honey

¼ teaspoon ground ginger

¼ teaspoon cinnamon

1 pound fresh cranberries, rinsed

Clean 12.5-ounce can or other vessel

In a medium saucepan, combine the apple cider, honey, ginger, and cinnamon. Bring to a boil over medium heat. Once boiling, reduce heat and simmer for 5 minutes.

Add cranberries to the pan and raise heat to medium. Bring to a boil and set timer for 15 minutes, stirring periodically. Do not boil more than 15 minutes or the pectin in the fruit will break down and sauce may not set properly.

Remove from heat and let cool for 5 minutes.

Spoon sauce into cans or other desired vessel. Refrigerate 4 hours or overnight.

When ready to serve, turn can upside down over a serving plate. Run a paring knife around the sides if necessary to loosen the sauce. Slice and serve.

Creamy Mashed Red Potatoes

with Garlic and Green Onions

12 red potatoes (about 2-pounds), cleaned with skins left on

½ cup unsalted butter, melted

½ cup half and half, heated but not boiling

2 cloves garlic, minced

¼ cup sliced green onions

½ teaspoon salt

½ teaspoon freshly ground black pepper

Additional butter, for serving

Bring a large pot of water to a boil. Cut potatoes in half or quarters so that all pieces are similar in size. Boil potatoes until fork tender, about 20 minutes.

Drain potatoes and transfer to the bowl of a stand mixer fitted with the paddle attachment. Let sit for a minute or two, allowing the steam to escape and the potatoes to dry slightly.

Add melted butter and beat on medium speed until butter is distributed. Add warm half and half, garlic, green onions, salt, and pepper. On medium speed, beat the potatoes until light and fluffy. Taste and adjust seasoning as needed.

Serve immediately.

Roasted Broccoli

2 crowns fresh broccoli, stemmed and cut into florets

Olive oil

1-2 teaspoons lemon juice

Kosher salt

Freshly ground black pepper

Preheat oven to 425°F.

Arrange broccoli on rimmed baking sheet. Drizzle with olive oil and lemon juice, tossing to coat. Sprinkle with salt.

Roast until broccoli is tender and just starting to char slightly, about 15 minutes.

Season to taste with salt and pepper.

Serve immediately.

Serving suggestions-
Grated Parmesan
Cheddar Cheese Sauce (Pg. 224)
Balsamic Glaze (Pg. 207)
Buttermilk Ranch Dressing (Pg.224)

"Good food is very often, even most often, simple food."
-Anthony Bourdain

Bacon Baked Beans

2 cups dried navy beans

1 teaspoon salt

¾ pound thick-slice bacon, chopped

1 medium onion, chopped

¼ cup ketchup

¼ cup brown sugar

2 tablespoons molasses

¼ cup pure maple syrup

2 teaspoons dry mustard powder

1 teaspoon freshly ground black pepper

Soak beans in a large bowl of water overnight. Drain.

Add beans and 1 teaspoon salt to a Dutch oven. Add enough cold water to cover the beans by 2-inches.

Bring to a boil, then reduce to a simmer, stirring occasionally, until beans are tender, about 35 minutes.

Drain and transfer beans to a bowl. Set aside.

Preheat oven to 250°F. Bring a kettle of water to a boil.

Heat Dutch oven over medium-high heat and cook the bacon until it just begins to brown. Turn off heat and add chopped onion, then top with beans.

In a small bowl, combine the ketchup, brown sugar, molasses, maple syrup, dry mustard, and pepper. Pour mixture over the beans and add enough of the boiling water to just cover the beans.

Cover pot with lid and bake 4-5 hours.

Remove pot from oven. Stir and season with salt to taste.

Return uncovered pot to the oven and bake an additional 45 minutes or until sauce has thickened and top is browned.

Serve immediately.

Sweet Potato Casserole
with Toasted Marshmallows

This recipe is one of the only times you'll see me list canned goods in the ingredient list. Can it be adapted to be made with fresh ingredients? You bet. Have I done it? Of course. Is it the same as the original that I grew up with? Not a chance. Our family firmly believes that one should never mess with the sweet potatoes. They're perfect just the way they are.

2 (40-ounce) cans Bruce's Yams, drained

1 ½ cups Crushed Pineapple in Juice, drained

½ cup brown sugar

4 tablespoons butter, melted

1 teaspoon salt

¼ teaspoon ground cinnamon

1 10-ounce bag mini marshmallows (or homemade, Recipe pg 236)

Preheat oven to 350°F.

In a large bowl, mash together the sweet potatoes, crushed pineapple, brown sugar, melted butter, salt, and ground cinnamon.

Spread mixture into a 9x13 baking dish.

Bake 30 minutes, or until heated through, stirring a few times. Top with mini marshmallows and return to oven until marshmallows are golden brown, about 10 minutes, rotating halfway through.

For best results, use homemade marshmallows (Recipe Pg.236), however if you're preparing the entire menu on Thanksgiving, please spare yourself the hassle and embrace store-bought and don't give it another thought.

Grilled Street Corn

While this recipe has decidedly Mexican roots, there's truly nothing quite like fresh Michigan sweet corn in the summer. This has become a favorite way to enjoy local corn ever since I took a trip to Texas and got hooked! I love serving it with fajitas or steak, preferably eaten outside at a picnic table with a paper towel in your lap. No need to be fancy. You'll want to shovel this corn into your mouth anyway.

8 ears fresh corn on the cob, husked

Canola oil

¼ cup mayonnaise

¼ cup sour cream

1 tablespoon lime juice

1 teaspoon chili powder

Pinch of cayenne pepper

Salt and pepper, to taste

½ cup crumbled queso fresco

¼ cup chopped fresh cilantro

Lime wedges, if desired

Husk corn and soak in water for 30 minutes while prepping the grill.

Preheat charcoal or gas grill for high direct heat. Brush corn with oil. Arrange corn on grill and cook until very lightly charred, turning as needed every few minutes. Transfer to a platter and let cool enough to handle and then remove corn kernels from the cob with a sharp knife.

In a medium bowl, combine corn kernels, mayonnaise, sour cream, lime juice, chili powder and cayenne. Taste and season with salt and pepper. Top with queso fresco and chopped cilantro.

Serve warm or room temperature with lime wedges if desired.

Grilling tip: If you would prefer not to char the corn at all while grilling, wrap in foil before grilling or gently peel back the husks. Alternatively, instead of removing the husks, just peel them back and remove the silk, then close the corn back up in the husks before soaking in water and grilling with the husks on.

"One of the very best things about life is the way we must regularly stop whatever it is we are doing and devote our attention to eating."

-Luciano Pavarotti

Main Courses

Mushroom & Swiss Sliders

2 tablespoons olive oil

12-ounces fresh sliced mushrooms

Salt, to taste

1-ounce dried mushrooms, chopped fine*

1.5 pounds ground chuck

1 tablespoon Worcestershire sauce

¾ teaspoon salt

¾ teaspoon freshly ground black pepper

Canola oil

Sliced onion, optional

Sliced Swiss cheese

Slider-sized pretzel buns (Recipe pg.44)

Heat olive oil in a large skillet over medium heat. Add sliced mushrooms and sauté until lightly browned. Remove from heat and set aside.

Heat a charcoal or gas grill for high direct heat.

In a large mixing bowl, combine dried mushrooms, ground beef, Worcestershire, salt, and pepper. Using clean hands, shape into patties about ¾-inch thick and 4-inches in diameter for sliders. (If making full size burgers, form patties to your desired size.) Press an indentation into the center of the patties with your thumbs to help ensure a flat burger once cooked. Season burger patties on both sides with salt and pepper.

Brush burger patties with canola oil and arrange on grill, cooking about 3 minutes or until golden brown. Flip burgers over and grill an additional 3-4 minutes until golden or cooked to your desired doneness. Top with Swiss cheese during the last minute of cooking and place cover on grill to help cheese melt.

Slice pretzel buns and brush inside lightly with oil. Place on hot grill until toasted.

Assemble burgers. Top with sautéed mushrooms and sliced onion, if desired.

*See pg. 248 for ingredient sources.

Mom's Meatballs, A Love Story.

Growing up, these meatballs were in the regular rotation at our house. I spent most of my childhood growing up living with my mom and my brother, just the three of us. Those years were difficult in a lot of ways, but also some of my most cherished memories. My mom was a single-parent, putting herself through college as an adult, and working less-than-glamorous jobs to give us the life she dreamt for us. Somehow in the midst of those difficult days, she managed to put delicious homemade meals on the table for us. At the time, I'm sure we probably nagged her for pizza or macaroni and cheese more than we should have, not realizing the act of love she was showing us through her food. To this day, I am transported back to my childhood dining room chair. The swinging kitchen door to my right, the creak of the porch swing coming from my left, and my brother by my side as always. We were probably bickering over who got to choose the evening's television programming, but in my memory, those little annoyances are glazed over and replaced with nostalgia and a longing to recreate those homemade moments for my daughters. These are not meatballs that are meant for spaghetti and garlic bread. These are a stand-alone situation that work well as an appetizer. Or serve them alongside mashed potatoes, blueberry muffins, and canned peaches like we did when I was a little girl.

I remember watching my mom form these by hand in our yellow galley kitchen, and it was the only meatball I ever knew growing up. Fast forward until I was a college graduate working in the same office as my mom, and a breakroom conversation clamoring for the "kind of meatballs" these were led to my groundbreaking discovery… There's such a thing as store-bought-meatballs? I had never heard of them, much less ever eaten any but our co-workers had never heard of making them from scratch. We all learned a little something new that day, all with a mutual love for my Mom's Meatball recipe. I still have never bought pre-made meatballs (except for that one time at the Swedish furniture megastore), and it's all her fault. Thanks Mom.

Mom's Meatballs

For the Meatballs:

1 ½ pounds ground chuck

1 ½ cups uncooked quick oats

2 tablespoons whole milk

½ teaspoon salt

½ teaspoon garlic salt

¼ teaspoon freshly ground black pepper

1-2 tablespoons olive oil

For the Sauce:

16 ounces tomato sauce

2 tablespoons white vinegar

2 tablespoons Worcestershire sauce

¼ cup brown sugar

In a large bowl, combine beef, oats, milk, salt, garlic salt, and pepper by hand. Shape into balls, about 1 ½ inches in diameter.

In a medium bowl, mix tomato sauce, vinegar, Worcestershire sauce, and brown sugar until combined. Set aside.

Heat olive oil in a large skillet over medium heat. Cook meatballs, turning frequently, until browned on all sides. Drain excess fat from pan. Add sauce mixture to pan and bring just to a boil, then cover and reduce heat to maintain a simmer. Continue simmering meatballs in sauce for 1 ½ hours. Serve hot.

Serving suggestions- Creamy Mashed Red Potatoes (Recipe pg. 88), and Roasted Broccoli (Recipe pg. 90).

Note- After meatballs are browned, they can be transfered to a slow cooker. Add the sauce mixture and set slow cooker to low heat for 4 hours, stirring occasionally to ensure even cooking.

All that I am or hope to be, I owe to my mother.
-Abraham Lincoln

Grilled Asparagus & Salmon Fillets
with Balsamic Glaze

¾ cup balsamic vinegar

2 tablespoons pure maple syrup (Grade B or dark amber Grade A)

1 tablespoon Dijon

1 clove garlic, minced (about 1 teaspoon)

4 salmon fillets with skin on one side

Olive oil

Salt & pepper, to taste

1 bunch fresh asparagus

Prepare the glaze. In a medium saucepan, combine balsamic vinegar, maple syrup, Dijon, and garlic over medium heat. Bring to a boil, stirring frequently, then reduce heat to low and simmer until thickened and reduced by half, about 20 minutes. Remove from heat and set aside.

Preheat a charcoal or gas grill for direct medium heat. Gather tongs, spatula, and serving platter. The entire grilling process only takes about 10-12 minutes, so be prepared to work quickly.

Toss asparagus with a few tablespoons of olive oil, until lightly coated. Season with salt and pepper.

Arrange asparagus around the perimeter of the grill, leaving space in the center for the salmon fillets.

Brush salmon fillets with olive oil and season with salt and pepper. Place salmon skin-side up in center of grill until grill marks appear, about 3 minutes.

Turn asparagus as needed to ensure even cooking. Test for tenderness by poking stalks with the tip of a sharp knife.

Carefully flip salmon fillets over and grill skin-side down until cooked through and salmon flakes easily, about 3-5 more minutes depending on the thickness of the fillets.

Transfer asparagus and salmon to serving platter. Salmon skin can be removed prior to serving. Drizzle with warm balsamic glaze and serve.

Beef Tenderloin
with Creamy Mushroom Sauce

4 tablespoons unsalted butter, divided

2 tablespoons canola oil, divided

16 ounces fresh mushrooms, sliced

3 tablespoons minced shallot

2 pounds beef tenderloin

¼ cup dry white wine*

¾ cup low-sodium beef stock

1 cup + 1 tablespoon heavy cream

2 teaspoons corn starch

Sea salt

Freshly ground black pepper

Egg noodles, for serving (Recipe pg. 124)

Heat 2 tablespoons butter and 1 tablespoon oil in a large skillet over medium heat until melted. Add mushrooms and sauté until lightly browned, about 7 minutes. Stir in shallots and cook for a minute longer. Season to taste with salt and pepper. Transfer to a bowl and set aside.

Remove fat from beef tenderloin and cut meat into pieces about 1 ½-inch cubes. Pat each piece dry with paper towels and set aside.

Add remaining butter and oil to skillet set over medium-high heat. Sauté beef a few pieces at a time until browned on the outside but not cooked through, about 3 minutes per side. Transfer cooked beef to a dish and set aside. Discard drippings from skillet.

Slowly pour the wine and stock into the skillet and bring to a boil over medium-high heat, scraping the bottom of the skillet with a wooden spatula to loosen the browned bits. Continue boiling until liquid has reduced to by slightly more than half. Pour in one cup of heavy cream.

Mix remaining tablespoon of heavy cream with corn starch in a small bowl until smooth. Add to skillet and simmer for about two minutes, until sauce has thickened slightly. Add mushrooms back to skillet. Taste and add salt and pepper as needed, about 1 teaspoon salt and ½ teaspoon pepper. Reduce heat to low.

Return beef and any juices back to the skillet. Gently stir to coat the beef with the sauce. Cover the skillet and cook on low for just a few minutes to heat the beef and mushrooms through, being careful not to overcook the beef. Recommended doneness is medium-rare to medium.

Serve with buttered egg noodles and green beans on the side.

Michigan wine recommendations- Chateau Fontaine's Riesling or Chateau Chantal's Naughty White

"The shared meal elevates eating from a mechanical process of fueling the body to a ritual of family and community, from the mere animal biology to an act of culture."
-Michael Pollan

Maple Glazed Pork Loin

This recipe is a favorite in our house. The maple syrup brings a layer of flavor without being overly sweet. The cider vinegar and Dijon pack a tangy punch that balances everything out. Be prepared, the glaze is addicting. You have my permission to put it on all the things.

1.5-pounds pork tenderloin, trimmed of excess fat

½ teaspoon sea salt

½ teaspoon freshly ground black pepper

½ teaspoon dried sage

2 tablespoons unsalted butter

6 tablespoons pure maple syrup

¼ cup + 2 tablespoons apple cider vinegar, divided

2 teaspoons Dijon mustard

Pinch ground ginger

Preheat oven to 400°F.

Rub pork loin with salt, pepper, and sage.

Heat butter in a large skillet over medium-high heat. Sear pork until browned on all sides. Transfer pork loin to baking dish and cover with foil. Reserve skillet and browned bits.

Roast in oven for 25-35 minutes until 150°F internal temperature.

While pork is roasting, prepare the sauce. Add 2 tablespoons cider vinegar to skillet over medium heat, scraping up the browned bits left from searing the pork. Add maple syrup, remaining ¼ cup cider vinegar, Dijon mustard, and ginger. Continue cooking, stirring constantly, until reduced and thick and syrupy, about 5-10 minutes. Keep warm.

Return the cooked pork loin to the skillet with the sauce, turning several times until coated. Slice and serve.

Detroit Coney Dogs

Detroit Coney Dogs are a Michigan classic that has a rich history filled with a fair amount of competition. Most Coney Dog lovers are loyal to their favorite style. From Detroit Coneys to Flint Coneys, or between American Coney Island vs. Lafayette Coney Island in Detroit, everyone has their own opinion of which is the truly authentic coney dog. This is a homemade version of Detroit Coney sauce. It is my understanding that some Coney restaurants include beef heart in their coney sauce, but I wanted this recipe to include more readily-available ingredients for the average home cook.

3 tablespoons canola oil, divided

1 medium onion, finely chopped

1 red bell pepper, finely chopped

2 cloves garlic, minced

1 pound ground beef (chuck)

2 tablespoons all-purpose flour

¾ cup beef broth

2 ounces tomato paste

1 teaspoon apple cider vinegar

3 tablespoons hot sauce

1 ½ teaspoons chili powder

½ teaspoon sweet paprika

½ teaspoon cumin

½ teaspoon oregano

½ teaspoon kosher salt

¼ teaspoon freshly ground black pepper

Koegel Vienna Franks, *see note

Additional chopped onion, for serving

Yellow mustard, for serving

In a large skillet over medium-high heat, add 2 tablespoons oil, onion, and red bell pepper, cooking until tender. Add garlic and continue cooking just until lightly golden. Transfer to a bowl and set aside.

Heat remaining tablespoon of oil in skillet over medium-high heat. Add beef and cook until browned. Transfer beef to a bowl and set aside.

Drain all but 2 tablespoons of fat from the skillet. Whisk flour and fat together over medium heat, stirring constantly until golden but not browned. Slowly whisk in broth, tomato paste, vinegar, hot sauce, and seasonings. Continue whisking until smooth and boiling.

Reduce heat to medium-low to maintain a simmer. Return both the beef and the onion mixture to the skillet and stir until combined.

Simmer over medium-low heat for 1 hour, stirring occasionally.

Transfer mixture in batches to an electric blender and pulse until sauce is thick, somewhat smooth and only small chunks remain.

Serve with grilled hot dogs. Top with chopped onion and yellow mustard if desired.

If Koegel Viennas are unavailable, substitute other hot dog with natural casings.

Whole Roasted Chicken
with Red Wine and Balsamic

Roasting a whole chicken is one of those meals that I feel like yield a very high bang-for-your-buck. The presentation and flavor will fool your guests into believing that you invested much more time and energy into the meal preparation than you actually did. Don't worry, your secret is safe with me. A great way to elevate this recipe is by using a good quality Michigan wine both for cooking the chicken, but also for serving. A fresh, local, organic chicken is also very highly encouraged if you are able to get your hands on one.

2 tablespoons unsalted butter, very soft

2 tablespoons minced fresh rosemary (2 teaspoons dried)

3 cloves garlic, minced

1 teaspoon sea salt

1 teaspoon freshly ground black pepper

1 large onion, chopped

6-7 lb. roasting chicken, preferably fresh, local, and organic

½ cup dry red wine*

½ cup balsamic vinegar

Remove chicken from refrigerator. Pat skin dry with paper towel and let chicken come to room temperature for about 30 minutes.

Preheat oven to 350° F.

In a small bowl, combine butter, rosemary, garlic, salt, and pepper until smooth.

Scatter onions in the bottom of a roasting pan. Lay chicken on the onions breast side up. Gently loosen the skin on the breasts and thighs and rub rosemary mixture underneath.

Tuck wings under the chicken and tie drumsticks together with butcher's twine.

Combine wine and balsamic together in a bowl and pour over chicken.

Roast, uncovered, at 350°F for 2-2 ½ hours until instant read thermometer registers 170°F in the thickest part of the thigh. Cover with foil to slow the browning process if needed. Remove from oven and tent with foil for 15 minutes before carving.

Transfer pan drippings to a small bowl and skim fat as needed. Serve with chicken.

Michigan wine recommendations- Chateau Grand Traverse's Silhouette or Chateau Fontaine's Pinot Noir

Chicken Purses

This is a slight variation on my favorite meal from when I was growing up, using homemade astry instead of crescent rolls.. As kids, we always called them chicken teepees, but somewhere along the way we started calling them chicken purses and the name stuck. Now my daughter devours them just like I did.

2 tablespoons olive oil

Salt and pepper

1 pound boneless skinless chicken breasts

8 ounces cream cheese, softened

4 tablespoons unsalted butter, melted

½ cup chopped onion

½ teaspoon salt

¼ teaspoon freshly ground black pepper

⅓ cup milk, for brushing

1 large egg + 1 tablespoon water, lightly beaten

Hot water crust, half batch (Recipe pg.229)

Cheddar Cheese Sauce (Recipe pg. 224)

Preheat oven to 350°F. Line a rimmed baking sheet with parchment paper. Arrange chicken breasts on prepared baking sheet and brush with olive oil. Sprinkle with salt and pepper. Bake until cooked through, about 45 minutes. Allow to cool a few minutes, then shred chicken using two forks.

In a large bowl, combine cream cheese, melted butter, onion, salt, and pepper until smooth. Add chicken and stir until combined.

Line 2 rimmed baking sheets with parchment paper.

On a lightly floured surface, roll dough out thin and trim into eight 5-inch squares.

Spoon filling onto each square of dough and brush edges with milk. Bring corners of dough together in the center and pinch to seal. Pinch seams together to seal. Arrange on prepared baking sheets.

Repeat with remaining dough and filling.

Brush assembled chicken purses with egg wash. Bake at 350°F for 20-30 minutes until golden brown.

Prepare cheddar cheese sauce while chicken purses are baking. Keep warm.

Remove from oven and serve immediately with cheddar cheese sauce.

Mandy's Boeuf Bourguignon

The very first time I really fell in love with the process of cooking with wine was a Thursday. I was working 12 hour shifts in a dental office, but that particular day my entire afternoon of patients cancelled due to an impending blizzard. I was gifted with an afternoon at home and the inspiration to try an adventurous recipe from my bucket list. Julia's Boeuf Bourguignon. I happened to have the ingredients list with me written in my planner for just such an occasion, so I quickly shopped at the supermarket across the street from my office and raced home to lace up my apron and get to work. For those who have followed that recipe, you may remember that several recipes-within-a-recipe are involved, and the masterful attention to detail and descriptions of the technique required to recreate this French staple in an American home kitchen. I followed the recipes to the letter and somehow, with no previous experience cooking with wine, I managed to complete each step with confidence. By the end of the afternoon and into the evening, I was smitten. The techniques involved to create the layering of flavors are a simple to execute, but taste complicated and pure all at once. That was the first of many times we enjoyed Julia's version of Boeuf Bourguignon. This recipe is my own more basic (read: less intimidating) version of that famous dish.
.

2.5 lbs. lean beef roast

1-2 tablespoons olive oil

1 tablespoon unsalted butter

1 large onion, chopped

2 celery stalks, chopped

2-3 carrots, sliced

4 cloves garlic, minced

3 tablespoons all-purpose flour

2 cups dry red wine*

4 cups (1 quart) beef stock or low-sodium beef broth

2 dried bay leaves

½ teaspoon thyme

2 tablespoons unsalted butter

16 ounces fresh whole mushrooms, cleaned and quartered

Sea salt and freshly ground black pepper

Chopped fresh parsley, for serving

Cut the meat into large cubes, about 2-inches across. Season with salt.

In a large, enameled cast iron Dutch oven, heat olive oil and butter over medium-high heat. Cook the meat in batches, for several minutes on each side until deep golden brown and a crust forms. This step is only to sear the meat and lock in moisture, not to cook it through.

Remove browned meat to a plate and set aside. Add onion, celery, carrots, and garlic to the pot with the browned bits from cooking the meat. Add another tablespoon of olive oil if needed. Saute until onions are translucent and carrots are lightly browned. Season with salt and pepper.

Preheat oven to 275°F.

Return the meat to the pot. Sprinkle the flour over the meat and toss around until the flour has coated the meat and vegetables well. Continue cooking over medium heat, stirring constantly for 2 minutes until flour is cooked and lightly golden.

Slowly pour in the red wine, scraping the bottom of the pot to loosen up the brown bits. Add the beef stock and bring to a simmer. Add bay leaves and thyme.

Cover with lid and place in preheated 275°F oven for 2 ½-3 hours until meat is tender when pricked with a fork, checking occasionally to ensure that the liquid is gently simmering. Adjust temperature as needed to maintain a simmer.

Meanwhile, heat 2 tablespoons of butter in a skillet over medium-high heat. Add quartered mushrooms and cook until browned. Remove from heat and set aside.

When the stew comes out of the oven, remove the bay leaves and stir in the mushrooms. Bring to a boil, uncovered, and cook until sauce has thickened to your desired consistency.

Serve with chopped parsley and buttered potatoes, if desired.

Enjoy immediately, or allow to cool to room temperature before storing in refrigerator overnight for serving the next day.

Michigan wine recommendations- Chateau Grand Traverse's Silhouette or Chateau Fontaine's Pinot Noir

This recipe reheats really well. In fact, the flavors are best the second day.

Detroit Deep Dish Pizza

Detoit is known for a lot of things. Motor City. Motown. The Lions, Tigers, and Red Wings. The "Come-back City". If you haven't experienced Detroit-style deep-dish pizza though, you're missing out. The signature crispy cheesy crust is achieved by using a high-fat content aged Wisconsin brick cheese, and a blue steel deep dish pan, which were originally made by the same manufacturers who supplied the auto industry in Detroit as well. It was a very exciting day when I scored my very well-seasoned pans from a pizzeria that was closing down.

2 ½ cups bread flour

1 ½ teaspoons instant yeast

1 tablespoon kosher salt

1 cup lukewarm water, about 110°F

Olive oil for pan

12 ounces Wisconsin Brick Cheese, cut into ½-inch cubes**

Pizza sauce (Recipe pg. 219)

Sliced pepperoni

In the bowl of a food processor, add flour, yeast, and salt. Pulse to combine. Add water and process on low speed until dough forms a ball. Continue processing for an additional 30 seconds.

Transfer dough to a lightly oiled bowl. Cover and let rise until doubled in size, about 2 hours at room temperature.

Preheat oven to 550°F.

Brush a 9x13-inch blue steel Detroit Deep Dish pan with olive oil. Transfer dough to pan and stretch dough to cover as much of the bottom of the pan as possible. Cover pan with plastic wrap and let rest 15 minutes before stretching dough again to reach the corners of the pan.

Arrange pepperoni in an even layer on top of the dough. Scatter cubed cheese on dough all the way to the sides of the pan. Spread sauce in three lines down the length of the pizza, spaced evenly.

Place pan on the floor of the oven and bake for 13-17 minutes, until cheese is bubbling and browned around the edges.

Cut into squares and serve immediately.

**See sources on pg. 248 for where to purchase brick cheese online. If it is not possible to use Wisconsin brick cheese, a combination of mozzarella and white cheddar cheeses may be substituted. Use the white cheddar around the edges and the mozzarella toward the middle as the white cheddar melts and crisps better to create the signature crispy cheese crust.

Venison Goulash

1 ½ pound ground venison or beef

2 tablespoons olive oil

1 medium onion, chopped

4 cloves garlic, minced

3 cups water

30-ounces tomato sauce

28-ounces canned diced tomatoes

1 teaspoon dried oregano

2 dried bay leaves

1 ½ teaspoons sea salt

1 teaspoon freshly ground black pepper

½ teaspoon cayenne pepper

2 cups elbow macaroni, uncooked

In a large Dutch oven, brown the meat in the olive oil. Add onion and garlic and cook until onion is translucent. Season with salt and pepper.

Add water, tomato sauce, diced tomatoes, oregano, bay leaves, and cayenne pepper. Cover and simmer for 20 minutes, stirring occasionally. Stir in macaroni.

Cover and cook over medium-low heat for 25 minutes, stirring occasionally. Taste and adjust seasonings as desired.

Remove bay leaves. Serve immediately.

Homestyle Egg Noodles

I am well aware that making homemade pasta is not everyone's idea of a good time, however if you choose to give it a try, I don't think you'll be disappointed. My inner old-soul and the fact that I lived in Italy for a while makes me more inclined to the homemade pasta lifestyle than most. My daughter loves these egg noodles with just a bit of butter and parmesan. So do her Mama and Papa.

2 cups all-purpose flour

2 egg yolks

1 whole egg

2 teaspoons salt

In the large bowl of a stand mixer fitted with the dough hook, add the flour. Make a well in the center of the flour. Add yolks, eggs, and salt to the center. Stir to combine.

Using the dough hook, turn mixer to medium speed for 10 minutes. Cover bowl and let dough rest for 15 minutes.

Divide dough into 4 portions.

Roll each portion very thin on a floured surface. If dough begins to shrink back when rolling, cover and let rest 10 minutes before continuing.

Cut dough into ½-inch thick strips and arrange on a large tea towel or pasta rack.

Repeat with remaining portions of dough.

Let dry several hours.

Cooking method- Bring large pot of salted water to a boil. Add pasta and boil 12-15 minutes until tender. Drain and serve.

Grilled Whole Turkey

This method works perfectly well for turkey or chicken. By spatchcocking the bird, the grill is able to cook the whole bird through in a fraction of the time that roasting a whole bird in the oven requires. Plus, the depth of flavor from the charcoal grill is outstanding. Nothing boring about this turkey. Give it a try for Thanksgiving. The ample amount of available oven space will be an added reward.

Whole turkey, spatchcocked and brined (see pg. 240)

8 tablespoons unsalted butter, softened

Spatchcock and brine the turkey. Split turkey thighs and legs from the breast and wings. After brining is complete, bring turkey to room temperature.

Preheat charcoal grill for medium-high indirect heat. Be sure to have extra charcoal and charcoal chimney ready for replenishing coals as needed.

Arrange turkey breasts on preheated grill skin-side-up over indirect heat. Cover and cook for 20 minutes.

Add thighs and legs to the grill skin-side-up and replace cover. Grill another hour, checking temperature and basting with butter periodically. Turkey is done when temperature reaches 165°F in the thickest parts of the breasts and thighs. Adjust cook time as needed based on thermometer readings, as grill temperatures can fluctuate.

Transfer turkey to a serving platter and cover with aluminum foil. Let rest for 30 minutes before serving.

Note- Average cook time for a 15-pound turkey is about 1 ½ hours. Generally plan for about 30 minutes per 5 pounds. Do not judge doneness based on cook times. Always use a thermometer to ensure food has reached a safe temperature.

UP North Pasties

Pasties are the quintessential Up North food. Most Michiganders, particularly those from the Upper Peninsula, the U.P., can probably agree that when done right, pasties are an all-inclusive meal that feels like home. Where the natives get restless is when agreeing upon the proper accompanying condiment. There are two camps: Team Gravy and Team Ketchup. I'm not here to make enemies, so I'll just recommend that you serve both and avoid conflict in pursuit of the perfect pasty experience. For heaven sake though, please pronounce the name correctly: it's pass-tees. And don't skip the rutabaga. Trust me on this one. The flavor and texture is key to making these pasties amazing. This recipe makes a huge batch, between 12 and 18 large pasties, depending on how large you make yours. I typically freeze about 12 each time I make them. They reheat perfectly for a complete meal with no fuss.

1 recipe Hot Water Crust, chilled (Recipe pg. 229)

6-8 medium sized red potatoes, peeled and cubed into ¼-inch cubes (about 4 cups)

1 medium/large rutabaga, peeled and cubed into ¼-inch cubes (about 2 cups)

2-3 medium carrots, cubed (about 1 ½ cups)

1 sweet onion, chopped (about 1 ½ cups)

1 ½ pounds flank steak, cut into ½-inch cubes (*See note)

3 cloves garlic, minced

1 ½ teaspoons salt

1 teaspoon freshly ground black pepper

¼ cup butter, cut into small cubes

¼ cup heavy cream (for brushing pastry), optional

For the Gravy-

¼ cup butter

¼ cup flour

4 cups low-sodium beef broth, warmed

Salt and pepper, to taste

(Continued on following page...)

In a large bowl, combine potatoes, rutabaga, carrots, onion, flank steak, garlic, salt, and pepper.

Line 2 rimmed baking sheets with parchment paper or silpat baking liners. Preheat oven to 350°F.

Divide dough into 12-18 equal portions (or however many you would like to make). Roll each portion into a circle, about 8-inches in diameter. Place 1-1 ½ cups filling on one half of circle. Top with a few cubes of butter. Fold dough over the filling and press and crimp edges to seal. Arrange on prepared baking sheets. Brush tops with cream and cut a few slits in the top of each pasty. Repeat with remaining dough and filling.

Bake at 350°F for 1 hour, rotating baking sheets halfway through baking time. At the end of baking time, turn oven off but do not open the oven door for 30 minutes.

Prepare the gravy-

In a large skillet over medium heat, add the butter and heat until foaming stops. Sprinkle in the flour and stir constantly until flour has cooked but not browned. Very gradually add the warm stock to the skillet, whisking constantly. Bring to a gentle boil, stirring frequently until gravy has reduced and thickened slightly. Season to taste.

Serve pasties warm from the oven with gravy or ketchup.

Makes 12-18 large pasties.

**Note: In order to cube flank steak easily, place the beef in the freezer for about 30 minutes and then cut into ½-inch cubes.*

Pasties freeze and reheat really well. After baking, let pasties cool completely before wrapping each pasty securely in aluminum foil and placing in zippered freezer bags. To reheat, place foil-wrapped pasties in a 350°F oven for 45-60 minutes until heated through.

Leftover Thanksgiving Pasties

What's a Leftover Thanksgiving Pasty? Basically, a hand pie filled with all of your favorite leftovers, dipped in gravy. It's my favorite Black Friday meal.

1 half-batch Hot Water Crust, chilled (Recipe pg. 229)

Roast turkey, light or dark meat

Leftover stuffing, corn, green beans

Cranberry sauce

Sweet Potatoes with Toasted Marshmallows

Roll out dough according to UP North Pasties recipe. Fill with desired leftovers. Bake 350°F for 1 hour. Serve with gravy.

Table Manners

Table Manners are the proper
way to eat and socialize at
the family dinner table. If you
are a lost Barbarian (with the
table manners equal to mine) then
you have no need for table
manners. But I do because I
am civillized and have the
need for table manners at home
so I can practise my manners here
and use my skills when dining out.
Another reason for table manners
is to just be plain old polite,
if I'm eating eggs through my
nose, that won't look to appitizing
(especially if they are hard boiled) and
I'm not likely to get girlfrien
or a thankyou from my family.
In honor of my family I
would like to present this poem:

Table manners are respected!
Barbarians are rude!
Your appitite is protected!
and so is your food!

"Table Manners" by Michael McGovern, written around age 9.

Salsa Verde Chicken Enchiladas
with Sour Cream Sauce

½ pound boneless skinless chicken breasts, about 2 breasts

2 tablespoons olive oil

Salt and Pepper

2 cups salsa verde, divided (Recipe pg. 212)

¼ cup cream cheese, softened

2 cups pepper jack cheese, shredded and divided

8 flour tortillas (Recipe pg. 57)

3 tablespoons butter

3 tablespoons all-purpose flour

2 cups chicken broth

1 cup sour cream

Preheat oven to 350°F.

Line a rimmed baking sheet with parchment paper. Arrange chicken breasts on prepared baking sheet and brush with olive oil. Sprinkle with salt and pepper. Bake until cooked through, about 45 minutes. Allow to cool a few minutes, then shred chicken using two forks.

Spray a large baking dish with cooking spray. Spread ¼ cup salsa verde in bottom of baking dish.

In a large mixing bowl, combine chicken, 1 cup salsa verde, 1 cup pepper jack cheese, and the cream cheese. Mix until combined.

Spoon about ½ cup of chicken mixture onto each tortilla and wrap tightly. Arrange in prepared baking dish.

In a medium saucepan over medium heat, melt the butter. Add flour and cook, stirring constantly for about 1 minute until flour has cooked but not browned. Gradually add chicken broth, whisking until smooth before adding more, and bring to a gentle boil. Add ¼ cup salsa verde and whisk until smooth. Remove from heat and stir in sour cream.

Pour sauce over enchiladas so that tortillas are completely coated. Sprinkle remaining 1 cup of pepper jack cheese over the top.

Bake uncovered at 350°F for 20-30 minutes until lightly golden and the sauce bubbles.

Serve immediately with remaining salsa verde.

A Michigan Receipt for Cooking Brook Trout in Camp

-National Cookery Book for the Women's Centennial Committees of 1876

Having cleaned the fish, find a slender, flexible branch of a tree (not pine or its congeners); fasten the fish by its head to the end of the branch. Stick the other end into the ground at an angle that will allow the fish to hang in front of the fire, where it will get the most heat. Put a small piece of pork on its head, so that a little of the fat will run down on the fish. Place a piece of 'hard tack' under it, to catch the drippings. Keep it turning, so that both sides will cook alike. When sufficiently done, eat it with the hard-tack, and be very thankful for so good a meal.

Whole Trout Baked in Salt Crust

I first learned this technique while living in Italy where fresh seabass was plentiful and affordable. This has since become my favorite way to prepare trout fresh from the Pere Marquette River on weekends at our cabin. Give it a try when you've got guests, because the presentation is quite a spectacle. We typically use this preparation on rainbow trout and brown trout, although it can be applied to which-ever type of fish you would like, just be sure to remove the scales if you choose a scaly fish such as a bass.

4 egg whites, room temperature

2 cups kosher salt*

1 whole trout, cleaned and gutted **

Olive oil, for serving

Lemons, for serving

Preheat oven to 450°F.

In a large bowl, beat 4 large egg whites until stiff peaks form.

Fold in 2 cups of coarse grain kosher salt.

On a rimmed baking sheet or oven-proof serving platter, spread about ½ cup of the salt mixture.

Lay whole fish on top, then completely cover the fish with the remaining salt/egg mixture, spreading about ½- to ¾-inches thick.

Bake 25-30 minutes until salt crust is golden.

Crack open the shell and remove fish. Serve with good olive oil and lemon.

*Diamond Crystal brand kosher salt recommended.

**If you are able to have the fish cleaned and gutted when you purchase it, I would encourage you to take advantage of that. For tips on buying whole fish, see pg. 241.

Chicken Pot Pie

Chicken Pot Pie is the ultimate comfort food, in my humble opinion. I highly recommend bringing it to new moms, families in grief, friends who have just moved, or as a perfect Sunday night supper at home before the busyness of a new week begins.

4 boneless skinless chicken breasts, about 1 lb.

3-4 tablespoons olive oil salt and pepper

5 cups low-sodium chicken broth

2 chicken bouillon cubes

½ cup unsalted butter

1 medium onion, finely diced

½ cup all-purpose flour

¼ cup whole milk or heavy cream

2-3 carrots, peeled and sliced

1 ½ cups sweet corn kernels

1 cup frozen peas

1 Pie Crust, sugar omitted (Recipe pg. 228)

1 egg white, lightly beaten

Kosher salt, for sprinkling

Preheat oven to 350°F. Line a rimmed baking sheet with parchment paper. Arrange chicken breasts on prepared baking sheet and brush with olive oil. Sprinkle with salt and pepper. Bake until cooked through, about 45 minutes. Allow to cool a few minutes, then shred chicken using two forks.

In a medium saucepan, heat the chicken broth and bouillon cubes over low heat until bouillon has dissolved.

In a large, heavy-bottomed pot or Dutch oven, heat the butter over medium heat. Add diced onion and cook until translucent, about 10-15 minutes. Sprinkle flour over onions and stir constantly, cooking for 2-3 minutes until flour is cooked but not browned. Gradually add the warm broth to the pot, stirring constantly. Taste, and season with salt and pepper. Add milk, carrots, corn, peas, and chicken.

Continue cooking over low heat until sauce has thickened. Spread filling into an ovenproof casserole dish or deep-dish pie plate.

Heat oven to 375°F.

Roll out pie dough and top the pot pie with the crust, trimming and crimping the edges as needed. Brush top of crust with egg white and sprinkle with Kosher salt. Cut slits in the center of the crust to allow steam to escape.

Place pot pie on a rimmed baking sheet and bake 45 minutes to 1 hour, or until crust is golden brown and filling is bubbling.

Let rest 10 minutes before serving.

"We must have a pie.
Stress cannot exist in the presence of a pie."
–David Mamet

Desserts

Cherry Almond Bundt Cake	142
Banket	145
Hot Fudge Cream Puffs	146
Childhood Chocolate Chip Cookies	149
Dutch Apple Pie	150
Banana Cake with Caramel Frosting	152
Snickerdoodles	155
Salted Maple Pie	156
Mackinac Island Fudge with Toffee Bits	160
"Secret Ingredient" Tart Cherry Pie	163
Salted Maple Bourbon Caramels	166
Cut-Out Sugar Cookies	169
Cookie Icing	169
Blueberry Rhubarb Crumble	170
Beignets	174
Spiced Oatmeal Cake	176
Chocolate Malt Bundt Cake	181

Cherry Almond Bundt Cake

Cherry and almond are a power couple. They balance eachother out beautifully, and both are better when they're together. Apparently the origins of this pairing date back to a time when cherry pits were ground and used in recipes with tart cherries. The flavor of the ground pits was very reminiscent of almond, so from then on, they were a match made in dessert heaven. However this combination came to be, I'm here for it.

2 ½ cups + 2 tablespoons all-purpose flour

2 teaspoons baking powder

1 teaspoon salt

1 cup unsalted butter, room temperature

1 ¾ cups granulated sugar

3 large eggs, at room temperature

½ teaspoon pure vanilla extract

½ teaspoon almond extract

¾ cup buttermilk

3 cups tart cherries, cut in half (fresh, jarred, or thawed from frozen)

Preheat oven to 350°F.

In a medium bowl, whisk together 2½ cups flour, baking powder, and salt.

In the bowl of a stand mixer fitted with the paddle attachment, cream together the butter and sugar on medium-high speed for about 5 minutes until very light and fluffy. Reduce speed to low. Add eggs one at a time. Beat in vanilla and almond extracts.

With mixer still on low speed, add ⅓ of flour mixture, then ½ of the buttermilk, followed by another ⅓ of flour mixture, remaining buttermilk, and finally the remaining flour mixture.

Toss cherries and remaining 2 tablespoons flour in a bowl until cherries are coated.

Add cherries to batter and stir just until dispersed evenly.

Prepare a Bundt cake pan by spraying with baking spray or brushing with Pan Release. (See pg. 231)

Spoon batter into prepared pan and smooth top with spatula.

Bake at 350°F on center rack for 55-60 minutes, rotating halfway through baking time.

Let cake cool in pan for 15 minutes. Carefully run a sharp knife around the edges of the pan to loosen the cake from the pan before inverting pan over a wire rack to release the cake.

Let cake cool completely before glazing.

Prepare the glaze: Whisk together the confectioners' sugar, almond and vanilla extracts, milk, and butter until very smooth. Drizzle over cooled cake and top with sliced almonds.

Slice and serve.

For the Glaze-
2 cups confectioners' sugar
1 teaspoon almond extract
1 teaspoon pure vanilla extract
3 tablespoons milk
1 tablespoon butter, very soft
Sliced almonds, for topping

Banket

The love for banket (pronounced bun-ket) runs deep in my family. Truth be told, it took me decades to muster the courage to even try it. The name was weird and it didn't appear to contain fruit or chocolate. Thanks, but no thanks. As I grew older, I took advantage of the endless supply at our Christmas brunches at my parents' house, and paired with a hot cup of coffee, it really is one of life's simple pleasures. As with most pastries, I greatly prefer the homemade version for its balance of flavors and perfectly tender-but-not-dry crust. Some bakery versions have too powerful almond flavor, in my opinion. I prefer to pull the almond flavor from the almond paste instead of almond extract, as extract can be overpowering at times.

For the Dough-

2 cups all-purpose flour

1 cup unsalted butter, cubed

½ cup cold water

Milk, for brushing

2 tablespoons granulated sugar, for sprinkling

For the Filling-

1 ½ cups almond paste (12 ounces)

2 large eggs

¾ cup granulated sugar

¼ teaspoon pure vanilla extract

Pinch sea salt

Piping bag

In a large bowl, cut butter into flour until mixture resembles cornmeal. Add cold water and mix until dough comes together. Shape into a disc, wrap in plastic wrap, and refrigerate for 4 hours.

In the bowl of a stand mixer fitted with the paddle attachment, beat almond paste, eggs, ¾ cup sugar, vanilla, and salt until smooth. Cover and refrigerate for 4 hours.

Preheat oven to 450 °F. Line 2 rimmed baking sheets with parchment paper.

Divide chilled dough into 6 portions. Roll each portion out into 16-inch strips about 4-inches wide.

Place chilled filling into piping bag, cut corner off bag to make an opening about 1-inch in diameter.

Gently pipe filling in a line along the center of each strip of dough, leaving about 1-inch of dough at each end. Brush edges of dough with milk. Roll dough around filling, pressing along seams to seal. Fold and pinch ends to seal.

Arrange three rolls on each baking sheet. Brush lightly with milk, then sprinkle with remaining 2 tablespoons of sugar.

Bake at 450°F for 14 minutes, rotating halfway through to ensure even browning.

Let cool completely before serving.

Hot Fudge Cream Puffs

½ cup unsalted butter

½ cup water

½ cup whole milk

2 teaspoons granulated sugar

¼ teaspoon salt

1 cup all-purpose flour

4 large eggs, beaten

Piping bag or large food storage bag with corner cut off

Ice Cream, preferably Hudsonville Golden Vanilla

Sanders' Hot Fudge Sauce, or homemade (Recipe pg. 222)

In a medium saucepan, combine butter, water, milk, sugar, and salt over medium heat until simmering, stirring constantly.

Add flour to pan and stir until a ball of dough forms. Continue stirring dough for 1 minute to allow the flour to cook.

Turn off heat. Transfer dough to the bowl of a stand mixer fitted with a paddle attachment. Let cool for a few minutes, then turn mixer on low speed and slowly add beaten eggs in a few additions, allowing mixture to combine before adding more egg. Not all beaten egg will be needed in order to achieve the desired texture for the dough. Mixture should be thick, smooth, and have a glossy appearance. There will likely be a few tablespoons of beaten egg leftover.

Preheat oven to 400°F.

Line 2 rimmed baking sheets with parchment paper and brush with water. This step brings humidity to the oven to encourage the pastry to rise.

Transfer dough to piping bag and pipe dough into mounds about 2-inches in diameter. Using a damp finger, dab the top of the mounds to smooth the pointed peaks.

Bake at 400°F for 20 minutes, then lower temperature to 350° for 10-15 minutes more until golden. DO NOT OPEN OVEN DURING BAKING PROCESS.

Transfer to wire rack to cool completely before filling.

Split pastries open and fill with ice cream. Top with hot fudge and serve.

Unfilled pastries can be frozen in an airtight container for up to 2 months.

As kids, my brother and I had the good fortune to be "adopted" as grandchildren by a dear elderly couple who were close friends of our parents'. Grandpa and Grandma Horton had us over every Sunday evening for ice cream, and in the summer months, we would get to go swimming in the pool at their condo. When the time came for the sundaes to be served, grandpa transformed their basement laundry room into his own little ice cream parlor, complete with 5 gallon barrels of golden vanilla Hudsonville ice cream and all the Sanders' hot fudge and caramel sauce that you could ever hope for. This recipe is for Grandpa and Grandma Horton, who lived a good part of their lives in the Detroit area, and were loyal Sanders' Chocolates supporters, of which Hot Fudge Cream Puffs is a specialty. I never had the opportunity to go to Sanders' for Hot Fudge Cream Puffs with them, but I have already made the trip with my oldest daughter and I look forward to telling her all about Grandma and Grandpa's basement ice cream parlor someday.

Today me will live in the moment.
Unless it's unpleasant in which case me will eat a cookie.
-Cookie Monster

Childhood Chocolate Chip Cookies

These cookies and I go way back. The Cookie Monster attended my 5th birthday. I looked outside at my party and he was sitting on our porch swing. I didn't put two and two together that my dad was mysteriously out of sight during the special guest's appearance until I was in my twenties.

½ cup unsalted butter, softened

½ cup shortening, room temperature

1 cup brown sugar

2 large eggs

1 teaspoon pure vanilla extract

2 cups all-purpose flour

1 teaspoon baking soda

1 teaspoon salt

2 cups semi-sweet chocolate chips

1 cup sweetened coconut flakes

1 ½ cups old-fashioned oats

1 cup white chocolate chips

Preheat oven to 375°F.

Line 2 rimmed baking sheets with parchment paper.

In the bowl of a stand mixer fitted with the paddle attachment, cream the butter, shortening, and brown sugar together on medium speed until light and fluffy, about 3 minutes.

Beat in eggs and vanilla until combined.

Add flour, baking soda, and salt, and mix to combine.

Add coconut, oats, and chocolate chips, mixing just until combined.

Scoop dough onto prepared baking sheets, about 2 tablespoons per cookie.

Bake at 375°F for 8-10 minutes until golden.

Let cool 5 minutes on baking sheet before transferring to wire rack to cool.

Note- These cookies are amazing warm, but I also have been known to stash some in the freezer and eat them while still frozen, and they're delicious.

Feel free to change up the mix-ins. There's no such thing as too much goodness packed into a chocolate chip cookie. Nuts, candy, toffee bits, anything goes!

Dutch Apple Pie

While we were living in Italy, Michael and I were invited to an Italian couple's home for dinner. Knowing that I enjoy cooking and baking, they requested that I bring an entree and a dessert that are very traditional American recipes. I chose to bring Chicken Pot Pie (Recipe pg. 139), and this Dutch Apple Pie.

Pie crust for a single-crust pie (Recipe pg.228)

7-8 apples peeled and thinly sliced **

½ cup sugar

½ teaspoon cinnamon

2-3 tablespoons brown sugar

For crumb topping-

½ cup sugar

¾ cup flour

1 stick unsalted butter, softened

Preheat oven to 400°F. Line a 9-inch deep dish pie plate with pie crust.

Peel and slice apples and place in a large bowl. Sprinkle with a tablespoon of lemon juice to prevent the apples from turning brown. Add sugar, cinnamon, and brown sugar. Gently combine with rubber spatula and spread apple mixture in to prepared pie crust.

In a medium bowl, combine topping ingredients with a pastry cutter or two forks until flour is mostly incorporated. Mixture will be crumbly. Carefully sprinkle topping over the apples, gently pressing down as needed to keep crumbles from falling off. Sprinkle with cinnamon, if desired.

Bake at 400°F for 40-45 minutes, until topping is golden. Allow to cool at least 30 minutes, preferably longer prior to serving to allow the juices to re-absorb into the apples. Enjoy!

**Note: I prefer to use variety of apples when baking apple pies.. Cortland, Empire, Ida Red, Granny Smith, Northern Spy, and Paula Red are all great baking apples that tend to hold their shape well and provide good flavor.

Banana Cake with Caramel Frosting

For the Cake-

2 tablespoons softened butter or cooking spray

2 tablespoons all-purpose flour, for pan

3 cups all-purpose flour

1 ½ teaspoons baking soda

1 ½ teaspoons salt

¾ cup unsalted butter, softened

2 cups + 2 tablespoons sugar

3 large eggs

2 teaspoons pure vanilla extract

1 ½ cups buttermilk

1 ½ cups mashed overripe bananas

1 cup chopped walnuts, optional

For the Frosting-

½ cup unsalted butter, softened

1 cup dark brown sugar

⅓ cup heavy cream

1 tablespoon pure vanilla extract

16 ounces confectioners' sugar

½ cup walnuts, roughly chopped

Preheat oven to 275°F. Grease a 9x13-inch metal baking pan with butter or cooking spray, then sprinkle with flour, tapping off excess flour. If using a glass pan, increase temperature by 25 degrees.

In a medium bowl, sift together the flour, baking soda, and salt.

In the bowl of a stand mixer fitted with the paddle attachment, cream together the butter and sugar until light and fluffy. Add eggs and vanilla and beat until smooth.

Add flour mixture and buttermilk to the butter mixture in alternating additions, beginning and ending with flour. Stir in bananas and walnuts.

Spread into prepared pan. Bake 1 hour, until tooth pick inserted into center comes out clean.

Let cool completely before frosting.

Prepare the frosting-

In a medium saucepan, melt butter over medium-low heat. Add brown sugar and cream, stirring until sugar has dissolved. Turn off heat and add vanilla.

Transfer to the bowl of a stand mixer fitted with the whisk attachment. Add confectioners' sugar and beat until very smooth. Thin as needed with additional cream.

Spread over cooled cake and top with chopped walnuts and sliced banana, if desired.

Snickerdoodles

½ cup unsalted butter, at room temperature

½ cup shortening, at room temperature

¾ cup sugar

½ cup brown sugar

1 large egg + 1 yolk

2 teaspoons pure vanilla extract

2 ¾ cups all-purpose flour

1 teaspoon baking soda

1 teaspoon cream of tartar

1 teaspoon salt

1 teaspoon cinnamon

¼ cup sugar

1 tablespoon cinnamon

Preheat oven to 325°F. Line 2 rimmed baking sheets with parchment paper. Position rack in center of oven.

In the bowl of a stand mixer fitted with the paddle attachment, cream together the butter, shortening, sugar, and brown sugar until light and fluffy, about 3 minutes.

Add egg, yolk, and vanilla and beat until combined.

In a medium bowl, whisk together flour, baking soda, cream of tartar, salt, and cinnamon.

Add flour mixture to butter mixture and mix just until combined.

In a small bowl, combined the remaining sugar and cinnamon.

Shape dough into balls, about 1 ½ inches in diameter and roll in cinnamon-sugar mixture.

Arrange on prepared baking sheets, leaving about 2-inches between each ball of dough.

Bake in two batches on rack in center of oven for 10 minutes until lightly golden around the edges. Cool on baking sheet 10 minutes before transferring to a wire rack to cool completely.

Note: Cookies will be quite puffy when they come out of the oven, but will flatten and gain their signature cracked appearance as they cool.

Makes 20-24 cookies.

Salted Maple Pie

Similar in texture to a pumpkin pie, but packed with way more flavor! Truly one of my very favorite recipes. Try making it for your next holiday party for a little something unexpected, or to celebrate the first batch of homemade syrup for the season, or my personal favorite, Pi Day, March 14.

1 ¼ cups pure maple syrup (dark amber or grade B)

¼ cup brown sugar

6 tablespoons unsalted butter, cut into pieces

½ cup heavy whipping cream

1 teaspoon pure vanilla extract

2 tablespoons all-purpose flour

2 tablespoons white cornmeal

¼ teaspoon salt

2 large eggs + 1 yolk, lightly beaten

Flaky sea salt, such as Maldon

1 blind-baked pie crust, cooled completely (Recipe pg. 228)

Preheat oven to 350°F.

In a medium saucepan, heat maple syrup and brown sugar over medium heat just until boiling, swirling the pan but not stirring. Remove from heat and stir in butter until melted. Add cream and vanilla, stirring until combined. Remove ½ cup of mixture to a small bowl and whisk in the flour, cornmeal, and salt. Add back to saucepan. Whisk in eggs and yolk until smooth.

Pour mixture into par-baked crust and bake at 350°F for 45-60 minutes until edges are just set and center still jiggles slightly. Cover edges of crust with foil if needed to prevent over-browning.

Let cool completely. Sprinkle with flaky salt before serving.

Makes one 9-inch pie.

Mackinac Island

Visiting Mackinac Island is something every visitor and resident of Michigan should do at least once in their lifetime, although once you've been there, it's hard not to go back repeatedly. Setting foot on the island is taking a step back in time. Transportation on the island is predominantly bicycles, walking, or horse-drawn carriage. No vehicles allowed. It's so charming. Darling little streets lined with boutiques and fudge shoppes are set against the backdrop of the stunning lake-shore views. The experience is like none other in this incredible state. Mackinac Island Fudge is a work of craftsmanship that has been a decadent symbol of the island for generations. Each fudge maker on the island seems to be quite secretive about their signature recipe, understandably, which made my research for this recipe a complicated and glorious task that I was thrilled to take on. First thing first, sample! In order to properly taste test and research, I ordered several blocks of fudge from various shoppes on the island. At the end of my 3-week long testing process, my husband did a blind side-by-side taste test and mine won! The silky smoothness achieved by following the scraping and turning process of slowly cooling and incorporating air into the fudge is the key to achieving the perfect texture in your homemade Mackinac Island Fudge. (Recipe on following page.)

Mackinac Island Fudge
with Toffee Bits

2 cups granulated sugar

¾ cup light brown sugar

4 ounces unsweetened chocolate, chopped

2 tablespoons unsweetened cocoa

1 cup heavy cream

1 tablespoon light corn syrup

Pinch kosher salt

5 tablespoons unsalted butter, room temperature

1 teaspoon pure vanilla extract

¾ cup toffee bits

Canola oil for brushing pan

Large surface for scraping and spreading fudge, preferably marble or granite (not wood)

Flat spatula, pastry scraper, or putty knife

Digital instant-read thermometer or candy thermometer

Brush a large heavy-bottomed saucepan with oil. Add sugar, brown sugar, chocolate, cocoa, cream, corn syrup, and salt to pan.

Heat over medium-high heat, stirring almost constantly until temperature reaches 235°F. Remove from heat and stir in vanilla. Dot surface of mixture with the butter and DO NOT STIR while mixture cools to 120°F.

Once mixture has cooled to 120°F, stir until butter has combined, then stir in toffee bits. Pour out onto marble board, scraping and folding mixture over onto itself until it loses its glossiness. This process of scraping and folding introduces air into the mixture and cools the fudge slowly for a perfectly smooth texture.

Shape into loaf and slice into 1-inch thick slices. Let cool completely before wrapping with waxed paper or parchment and storing in an airtight container at room temperature for up to 2 weeks or in the freezer for up to 6 months. Let come to room temperature before serving.

Visit: kitchenjoyblog.com/fudge-video *to see me demonstrate this recipe.*

"Secret Ingredient" Cherry Pie

Tart cherries are my love language. At any given time, I have a minimum of 5 pounds of pitted tart cherries in my freezer from a local orchard for those just-in-case moments throughout the year when the mood strikes for an epic cherry pie, which is more often than one might think.

I use frozen pitted tart cherries in this recipe because they're much easier to find for most people who don't live near cherry orchards like I do. Have no fear- this method yields a perfectly thickened filling every time. No more soupy pies! The secret ingredient of almond paste adds a layer of flavor and also helps avoid the dreaded soggy bottom that fruit pies can sometimes suffer from. Basically, it brings me joy.

2 pounds frozen pitted tart cherries

1 cup light brown sugar

¼ cup cornstarch

1 tablespoon bourbon

¼ teaspoon salt

5 tablespoons almond paste, at room temperature

1 egg white + 1 tablespoon cold water, lightly beaten

Raw sugar for sprinkling

Pie crust for double-crust pie, chilled at least 4 hours

Preheat oven to 425°F.

Line a 9-inch pie plate with pie crust. Roll out pie dough for top of pie. Cut into strips if doing a lattice crust. Lay out on a lightly floured baking sheet and cover with plastic wrap. Place pie plate and baking sheet in refrigerator.

In a large microwave-safe bowl, combine the frozen cherries and the brown sugar. Microwave on high heat for 2 minutes, stir, then microwave for 2 minutes more or until cherries are thawed completely and just warm.

Add cornstarch, bourbon, and salt to cherry mixture, stirring to combine.

Remove pie plate lined with bottom crust from the refrigerator. Spread almond paste on bottom crust in an even layer. Top with cherry mixture.

Remove top crust from refrigerator and arrange on top of pie in desired design, crimping edges to seal. Brush crust with egg wash. Sprinkle with raw sugar.

Bake on center rack at 425°F for 20 minutes. Lower temperature to 350°F and bake for 35-45 minutes more, or until filling is bubbling steadily. Cover edges of crust with foil as needed to prevent over-browning.

Let cool completely, preferably overnight, before cutting. This ensures clean slices and a properly set filling.

Apple Blossoms, Michigan's State Flower

Salted Maple Bourbon Caramels

Maple syrup, sea salt. bourbon, and brown sugar...in bite-size caramel form. What are you waiting for?

1 cup heavy cream

¼ cup bourbon

5 tablespoons unsalted butter

1 teaspoon vanilla

¼ cup water

6 tablespoons brown sugar

¼ cup granulated sugar

½ cup pure maple syrup (preferable dark amber or grade B)

1 teaspoon sea salt

Flaky sea salt, for sprinkling

Line an 8x8-inch baking pan with parchment paper.

In a small sauce pan, combine the cream, butter, bourbon, and vanilla. Simmer over medium-low heat until butter has melted.

In a large saucepan fitted with a candy thermometer, add water, brown sugar, granulated sugar, maple syrup, and sea salt. Do not stir. Bring to a boil and just until sugar melts. Add cream mixture and continue cooking until temperature reaches 248°F.

Keep mixture at 248°F for about 30 seconds. This helps ensure that the caramels will set properly.

Very carefully pour hot mixture into prepared pan. Let sit 30 minutes at room temperature then sprinkle with flaky salt. Let cool completely before removing from pan by lifting up on the parchment paper. Cut into pieces using a very sharp knife, oiling the blade as needed to prevent sticking. Wrap caramels individually with parchment paper. Keep at room temperature or refrigerated.

Cut Out Sugar Cookies

4 cups all-purpose flour

1 teaspoon baking powder

½ teaspoon salt

2 sticks (1 cup) unsalted butter, softened

2 cups granulated sugar

2 large eggs

2 teaspoons pure vanilla extract

In a large bowl, whisk together flour, baking powder, and salt.

In the bowl of a stand mixer fitted with the paddle attachment, beat butter and sugar until light and fluffy, about 3 minutes. Beat in eggs and vanilla. With mixer on low, gradually add dry ingredients. Mix until combined. Divide dough in half. Flatten into disks. Wrap each disk in plastic wrap and refrigerate at least 4 hours.

Roll out dough on a floured surface and cut out cookies into desired shapes about ¼-inch thick and place on parchment-lined baking sheet. Place sheets in freezer for 10-15 minutes before baking.

Preheat oven to 325°F.

Move baking sheets from freezer directly to oven and bake on center rack until edges are just beginning to look golden and the surface of the dough has lost its sheen, about 11-14 min. depending on the thickness of the dough.

Let cool completely before decorating.

Cookie Icing

4 cups confectioners' sugar, sifted

¼ cup light corn syrup, plus more as needed

½ cup milk, plus more as needed

gel food coloring

½ teaspoon pure vanilla extract (omit for bright white icing)

In the bowl of a stand mixer fitted with the whisk attachment, combine confectioners' sugar with ¼ cup of the milk and 2 tablespoons light corn syrup. Beat on medium speed until smooth. If needed, add remaining milk and light corn syrup to achieve a thick yet pourable and slightly glossy consistency. Icing should drizzle slowly from a spoon. Divide icing into bowls and add coloring as desired.

Icing can be piped or spread onto cooled cookies. To pipe, trace an outline with the icing, then thin out some of the icing with a bit of corn syrup. "Flood" the center with the thinned icing and spread with a toothpick. Let icing harden at room temperature before serving.

Blueberry Rhubarb Crumble

This is one of those desserts that I love to make on Summer nights when it is too hot be inside with the oven on, so you have to escape to the backyard and play outside a little longer.

For the Filling-

1 ½ tablespoons unsalted butter

5 cups fresh blueberries**

2 cups rhubarb, chopped

½ cup granulated sugar

¼ cup brown sugar

3 tablespoons all-purpose flour

2 tablespoons lemon juice

Pinch salt

¼ teaspoon cinnamon

Pinch allspice

For the Topping-

2 cups old-fashioned oats

½ cup granulated sugar

¼ cup brown sugar

¼ teaspoon salt

¾ teaspoon cinnamon

1 stick (½ cup) unsalted butter, melted

½ teaspoon pure vanilla extract

Preheat oven to 350°F.

Butter a 2-quart baking dish or 9x9-inch baking pan.

In a large bowl, combine blueberries, rhubarb, granulated sugar, brown sugar, flour, lemon juice, salt, cinnamon, and all spice. Stir until fully incorporated.

Pour filling mixture into prepared baking dish and bake for 30 minutes.

While filling is baking, prepare the topping. In a medium bowl, stir together the oats, granulated sugar, brown sugar, salt, cinnamon, melted butter, and vanilla together until evenly distributed.

Spread topping mixture over the filling and bake an additional 45 minutes until topping is golden and filling is bubbling and syrupy in appearance.

Let cool 15-30 minutes before serving to allow filling to set up.

Serve warm with vanilla ice cream.

**Frozen blueberries can be substituted by microwaving the berries 3-4 minutes until thawed and just warm.

Beignets

½ cup lukewarm water

1 envelope (2 ¼ teaspoons) instant yeast

½ cup evaporated milk

1 egg, room temperature

1 teaspoon pure vanilla extract

2 tablespoons canola oil

¼ cup granulated sugar

1 teaspoon sea salt

3 cups all-purpose flour

Canola oil, for frying

Confectioners' sugar, for dusting

Digital instant-read thermometer or fry thermometer

Fine mesh sieve or frying spider

Large heavy-bottomed saucepan

Warm Vanilla Sauce, for serving**

Raspberry Coulis, for serving**

Warm Nutella Sauce, for serving**

Prepare sauces, if desired. Keep warm while making the beignets.

In a large bowl, add water and yeast. Add evaporated milk, egg, vanilla, oil, sugar, and salt. Whisk to combine. Mix in flour, beating until thoroughly combined and a sticky dough forms.

Add enough oil to a large heavy-bottomed saucepan so that it is about 2-inches deep. Heat oil over medium-high heat to 370°F, adjusting heat as needed to maintain temperature.

On a floured surface, roll out one-third of the dough to ¼-inch thickness using a floured rolling pin. Cut dough into squares or other desired shape about 2-inches by 2-inches.

Gently drop 3-4 squares of dough into hot oil, one at a time, watching the thermometer closely. If the temperature drops below 370°F, wait until the temperature comes back up before adding any more dough to the oil. Cook dough in hot oil for about 1 ½-2 minutes, until golden and puffed up before using a mesh sieve to flip dough over. Cook the second side until golden, about 2 more minutes.

Drain on paper-towel lined platter. Repeat with remaining dough until all beignets are cooked, continuously adjusting the heat to maintain temperature. If the oil isn't hot enough, the beignets will turn out heavy and oily. If too hot, they will be done on the outside but uncooked inside.

Sprinkle beignets generously with confectioners' sugar and serve warm with desired sauces.

Note- Dough can be prepared and refrigerated for up to 3 days prior to frying. Let come to room temperature before frying.

**See pg. 216 for sauce recipes.

When Michael and I were newly married, we shared many a relaxing brunch during our travels and if beignets were on the menu, they were absolutely at the top of my list of things to order. These homemade beignets are even better than those made in a restaurant. They're so incredibly decadent, and if you're diligent at monitoring the oil temperature you'll avoid the final product turning out chewy or oily. They're foolproof, tender, fluffy, and completely out of this world when paired with my favorite trio of accompanying sauces: Nutella sauce, Vanilla sauce, and Raspberry coulis.

Spiced Oatmeal Cake

Oatmeal isn't just for breakfast anymore. Although this cake does make a pretty great breakfat, especially when served on my Grandma's china. The buttery, slightly crunchy coconut topping is what dreams are made of... at least mine are.

For the Cake-

1 ½ cups old-fashioned oats

1⅓ cup boiling water

½ cup unsalted butter, softened

1 cup granulated sugar

1 cup light brown sugar

1 teaspoon pure vanilla extract

3 large eggs, at room temperature

1 ½ cups all-purpose flour

1 teaspoon baking soda

½ teaspoon baking powder

½ teaspoon kosher salt

1 ½ teaspoons cinnamon

½ teaspoon nutmeg

Preheat oven to 350°F. Spray a 9x13-inch baking pan with nonstick cooking spray or brush with butter.

Combine oats and boiling water in a heatproof bowl. Let set 20 minutes.

In a medium bowl, whisk together the flour, baking soda, baking powder, salt, cinnamon, and nutmeg. Set aside.

In the bowl of a stand mixer fitted with a paddle attachment beat the butter with the granulated sugar and brown sugar for 3-5 minutes.

Add eggs, one at a time, mixing until smooth. Add vanilla and oat mixture, mixing until oats are evenly disbursed. Pour flour mixture into butter mixture and mix on low speed just until combined.

Spread batter into prepared pan. Bake 40-45 minutes until toothpick comes out clean.

Prepare the topping. Combine melted butter with brown sugar, milk, vanilla, and coconut.

Remove cake from oven and turn on broiler. Immediately spread topping mixture over top of warm cake. Place cake under the broiler for 2-3 minutes until topping is bubbling and slightly golden. Watch carefully to avoid the sugar from scorching.

Let cool at least 15 minutes before serving.

Serve plain or with a dollop of whipped cream and fresh berries.

For the Topping-

6 tablespoons unsalted butter, melted

1 cup brown sugar

3 tablespoons whole milk

1 teaspoon pure vanilla extract

1 cup sweetened coconut flakes

A Michigan Receipt for
Making Shortcake in Camp

-National Cookery Book from the Women's Centennial Committees of 1876

Take the top of your provision box, or one of the boards from the bottom of your boat (camp supposed to be on the shores of Lake Superior). As it will probably be rough, cover it with a napkin, then you have a good pasteboard. Get your Indian guide to find a smooth sapling, peel off the bark, scrape it smooth, and then you have your rolling pin. Mix half a pound of butter in half a pound of flour; but as you have probably left your scales at home, measure three or four tablespoonfuls of butter and one quart of flour; add a small spoonful of salt. Wet it with the coldest water you can get, roll it out about one-third of an inch thick, and of a shape suitable to your cooking utensil. If you are so luxurious as to have a camp-stove or baker, you can cut the paste into cakes and bake them as you would in civilized life; but if you take things after the manner of the aborigines, you will pour the grease from the frying-pan in which the salt pork has been cooked, and put the sheet of paste into it, cooking it over some coals drawn from the fire. There is still another way. If you can find a smooth, flat stone, heat it thoroughly in the fire; then withdraw it, and having dusted it with flour, bake your cake upon it. Eaten with a good mug of tea, a thin slice of pork, brown and crisp, and a broiled trout, all seasoned with good appetite, nothing can be more delicious.

For the Glaze-

4 ounces semi-sweet chocolate, finely chopped

1 ½ tablespoons light corn syrup

½ cup heavy cream

1 ½ tablespoons granulated sugar

1 ½ tablespoons malted milk powder

Chocolate Malt Bundt Cake

I feel very strongly that everyone needs a go-to chocolate cake recipe in their repertoire, and this is mine. I'm an unapologetic lover of Bundt® cakes and this chocolate cake is among my very favorite cakes to celebrate any occasion. Sour cream brings an added bit of moisture, which is most prominent the day after baking, so for that reason I recommend serving it on the second day. The addition of the malted milk powder brings a subtle layer of flavor to the richness of the chocolate. Topped with a chocolate ganache, just add some vanilla ice cream and this cake is party-ready.

For the cake-

1 cup unsalted butter

⅓ cup cocoa powder, plus more for pan

⅓ cup malted milk powder

1 teaspoon kosher salt

1 cup whole milk

1 ¾ cups granulated sugar

2 cups all-purpose flour

1 ½ teaspoons baking soda

2 large eggs, room temperature

½ cup sour cream, room temp (not nonfat)

1 teaspoon pure vanilla extract

In a medium saucepan set over medium heat, combine butter, cocoa, malt powder, salt, milk, and sugar until melted. Remove from heat and let cool slightly.

In a large bowl, whisk together flour and baking soda. Add cocoa mixture and whisk until combined. Add eggs, sour cream, and vanilla, whisking until smooth.

Prepare pan by spraying generously with baking spray or brushing with Pan Release. (See pg. 231)Sprinkle greased pan with cocoa powder.

Pour cake batter into prepared pan and smooth surface of batter with spatula.

Bake at 350°F for 40-45 minutes until toothpick comes out clean.

Let cake cool in pan for 10 minutes. Gently run a knife around the edges of the pan to loosen cake before inverting over a wire rack to cool completely.

When cake has cooled completely, prepare the glaze.

In a medium bowl, add chocolate and corn syrup.

In a small saucepan over medium heat, combine heavy cream, sugar, and malt powder until sugar has dissolved but not boiling. Remove from heat.

Pour cream mixture over chocolate and whisk until chocolate has melted and glaze is smooth. Let glaze cool a bit if necessary to reach a thick but pourable consistency.

Pour glaze over the top of the cooled cake. Serve.

"Would you like to have an adventure now, or would you like to have your tea first?

–Peter Pan

Drinks & Beverages

Homemade Root Beer	185
Cold Brew Coffee	186
Boston Coolers	189
Basil Lemonade	190
Apple Cider Sangria	192
Ginger Sweet Tea	194
Mulled Apple Cider	197

Homemade Root Beer

My hometown of Grand Rapids has been named Beer CIty USA twice, which led to a boom in the number of local craft microbreweries in our town. Drinking local has become a huge industry and way of life for many who live here. Home brewing is gaining in popularity as well. This homemamde root beer is my nod to our local beer industry, and is a very basic home brewing project that is sure to please even non-beer drinkers. No fancy brewing equipment is needed. Natural fermentation is used to carbonate this root beer, so there will be trace amounts of alcohol in the final product.

1 gallon + 3 ⅓ cups water

2 ½ cups granulated sugar

½ cup pure maple syrup

½ ounce root beer soda base *

½ teaspoon brewer's yeast *

2 clean plastic 2-liter pop bottles with caps **

Funnel

Instant-read thermometer

In a large stock pot, heat water to 180°F. Stir in sugar, maple syrup, and extract. Cool to 70°F.

Sprinkle brewer's yeast on top of liquid. Cover and let ferment until bubbles appear, about 12-24 hours.

Using a funnel, transfer root beer to bottles and store in a dark, warm place for 1-3 days. Longer fermentation results in more carbonation, alcohol, and a stronger flavor. Open caps once per day to release pressure. Transfer bottles to refrigerator to stop the fermentation process.

Refrigerate until ready to serve.

Serve cold in a chilled glass.

Root beer soda base and brewer's yeast can be found in home brewing supply shops and online. See pg. 248

**Do not use glass bottles for the fermentation process due to risk of shattering from the pressure buildup.*

Cold Brew Coffee

My husband and I are very interested in simple coffee-brewing methods, and cold brew is quite possibly the most simple method there is for making coffee. The result is a very smooth cup of coffee that when served over ice, is nearly unbeatable on those first warm Spring mornings in Michigan. You know the day. The one where suddenly the temperatures are in the 40's and everyone and their brother is driving with their windows down. Trust me. It's a thing. Ask anyone from Michigan. It's the happy day. The day that people are nicer than usual to strangers, and where we feel there might just be hope for a future without scraping ice from windshields and spending ten minutes bundling up just to walk to the mailbox. That's a day for cold brew.

1 cup ground coffee, ground for drip coffee (medium grind)

5 cups filtered water

1 paper coffee filter

2 large bowls

Fine mesh sieve

Pitcher or large jar with lid

Stir together the coffee grounds and water in a large bowl. Cover and refrigerate for 24 hours.

Line a fine mesh sieve with a coffee filter and set over a large, clean bowl.

Gradually pour the coffee through the filter set over the bowl.

Discard used coffee grounds. (Or use in your garden!)

Enjoy cold brewed coffee right away over ice, or seal in an airtight container and refrigerate for up to 1 week.

Note- Cold brew coffee is concentrated so that it does not taste watered-down when poured over ice. Feel free to dilute the coffee to your preferences with either water, milk, or creamer.

Boston Cooler

Don't let the name fool you...this frosty treat has nothing to do with Beantown. It is a Michigan creation through and through– specifically from Detroit. "Boston" refers to Boston Boulevard, the street near where James Vernor (inventor of Vernors) operated a pharmacy and soda fountain. While a Boston Cooler only requires two ingredients, it is very important that you choose those ingredients wisely and make no substitutions. In order to properly enjoy an authentic Boston Cooler you MUST use Vernors Ginger Ale, a Michigan-made favorite that has been known to cure all ailments in the land shaped like a mitten. Secondly, I highly recommend using Hudsonville ice cream, also made in Michigan. It's an unbeatable combination on a warm summer day.

3 scoops Hudsonville vanilla ice cream

12-ounces Vernors Ginger Ale

Add ice cream and ginger ale to the container of a blender. Blend until smooth. Enjoy!

Note- If you don't have a blender available, Vernors also makes a superb float.

Basil Lemonade

Fresh Basil adds a crisp, refreshing flavor to homemade lemonade with very little effort. If available, adding a handful of fresh strawberries with the basil makes this an extra special Summer drink.

1 cup fresh basil leaves

⅓ cup granulated sugar

8 cups water

1 cup fresh squeezed lemon juice

In the bottom of a large glass bowl, rub the basil and sugar together using a wooden spoon until basil leaves are mashed and combined with the sugar.

Pour water and lemon juice into the bowl with the basil mixture. Taste and adjust sweetness as desired.

Strain into pitcher of ice.

Serve chilled with lemon wedges or fresh strawberries for garnish.

Apple Cider Sangria

This Autumn sangria is great way to enjoy the first of the crisp apples from the Fall harvest. Sweet, tart, and slightly spicy all at the same time, it's a crowd pleaser for sure. Do yourself a favor and grab some sunflowers while you're at the Farmer's Market too.

1 -750mL bottle Michigan cherry wine*

2 cups fresh Michigan apple cider

1 ½ cups (12-ounces) Vernors Ginger Ale

½ cup orange juice

1 tablespoon Cointreau

4 cinnamon sticks

2-3 apples, peeled, cored and sliced

In a 2-quart pitcher, combine all ingredients and stir until combined.

Cover and refrigerate 4 hours.

Serve over ice.

Note: Traverse Bay Winery Cherry Wine, Round Barn Winery Cherry Wine, or Cherry Republic Balaton Cherry Wine all work well.

Ginger Sweet Tea

The very first time I made this recipe, it was early Spring at our first house. Our oldest daughter was only about 9 months old. I made a few test batches for Michael to sample and compare, and we sat outside in our yard while Addilyn got her first feel of grass beneath her feet. She was smitten with the ticklish green floor outside, to be sure. Every time I make this tea I am transported back to that first little Michigan kitchen of mine, and our sprawling yard dotted with stately maples. We outgrew that house over the years, but I surely am thankful for the incredible memories that were created there. The tea was pretty great too.

For the ginger syrup-

1 fist-sized piece of fresh ginger, peeled and sliced very thin (to equal about 1 cup)

1 cup granulated sugar

1 cup water

For the iced tea-

5 teabags of Lipton black tea

2 cups boiling water

6 cups ice cubes

In a medium saucepan, combine fresh ginger, sugar, and water. Bring to a boil over medium heat. Reduce to a simmer. Cook for 30 minutes, adjusting heat as needed to maintain a simmer, stirring occasionally. Mixture should be reduced by half.

Pour syrup through a fine mesh sieve to remove the ginger pieces. Let syrup cool to room temperature before sealing in a jar and storing in the refrigerator. (You don't need to let it cool in order to use it to make the tea. You'll only need half of the syrup to make a pitcher of tea.)

In a 2-quart glass pitcher, add the teabags. Pour boiling water over the teabags and let steep for 5 minutes. Remove teabags and add ½ cup of the ginger syrup, stirring to combine. Add ice, stirring well to cool the tea.

Serve cold.

Mulled Apple Cider

1 gallon fresh Michigan apple cider

2 large oranges, quartered

3 tablespoons whole allspice berries

1 ½ tablespoons ground cinnamon, or 4-5 cinnamon sticks

2 teaspoons cardamom

2 teaspoons nutmeg

In a large heavy-bottomed pot set over low heat, add the cider. Add the orange slices and seasonings. Simmer, but do not boil, for as long as you want. I like to let mine simmer for an hour or two. The flavors are more developed, and the house smells amazing.

Prior to serving, pour the cider through a fine-mesh sieve to filter out all of the allspice berries, etc.

Note- This can also be prepared in a slow cooker set on high for 2-3 hours.

"Waiter, I'll begin with the house salad, but I don't want the regular dressing. I'll have the balsamic vinegar and oil, but on the side, and then the salmon with the mustard sauce, but I want the mustard sauce on the side." "On the side' is a very big thing for you."

-When Harry Met Sally

Dressings, Dips, & Sauces

Homemade Maple Syrup

Maple trees, minimum 12-inches in diameter

Clean food-safe jugs, such as gallon milk or water jugs with caps

5/16-inch diameter food-grade vinyl tubing

Cordless drill

¼-inch diameter drill bit

Large stock pots

Outdoor heat source

Canola oil, for brushing pot rim

Strainer

Cheesecloth

Candy thermometer

Storage container for finished product

Identify the mature maple trees. Sugar, Black, Silver, and Red maples are all suitable maples for making syrup. Sugar Maples and Black Maples yield higher sugar content than Silver or Red Maples. Trees must be mature, or a minimum of 12-inches in diameter to be suitable for tapping. Tree identification is easiest in the Summer or Fall, before the leaves have fallen for the Winter.

Gather supplies ahead of time, as the sap will begin running as soon as weather conditions accomodate, generally around February or March. The trigger for the sap beginning to run is the first days where temperatures rise above freezing, but nighttime temperatures still fall below freezing. Monitoring the weather conditions and tapping the trees promptly is the best way to assure maximum sap collection.

Tap the tree. Drill a hole 2-2 ½ inches deep about 3 feet off the ground. Insert one end of tubing into tapped hole just deep enough that it doesn't fall out. Inserting the tubing deeper may block sap from entering tube and cause the sap to run down the side of the tree. Drill a hole into the cap of a clean gallon jug. Insert the other end of the tubing into the jug through the hole in the cap. If syrup is running, sap will flow through the tubing immediately.

Be sure to monitor sap collection throughout the day and empty the collection jugs as needed. Store sap in a cool, shaded area no warmer than 37°F. Transfer collected sap into remaining gallon jugs, using a fine mesh sieve lined with a flour sack towel to filter out any debris.

Prepare the heat source. If using a wood-burning fire pit, be sure to have sufficient wood available to burn for several hours.

Set large stock pots over heat source and fill ¾ full with sap. Brush the inside rims of the pots with Canola oil to help prevent sap from boiling over. Boil sap until pots are about ¼ full. Transfer boiled sap to a clean pot and set aside for final boiling to be done indoors. Repeat with remaining sap.

Final boil. Transfer all reduced sap to a smaller clean pot and bring into kitchen. Heat pot on the stove until boiling. Attach candy thermometer to pot and watch temperature very closely. Syrup will begin to take on a slightly thickened consistency and golden brown color. Continue boiling until temperature reaches 219°F (or 7° above boiling point if at high elevation).

Transfer syrup to a glass measuring cup or jar. Cover and refrigerate overnight. In the morning, there will likely be some sediment settled in the bottom of the jar. Carefully pour syrup into desired storage container without disturbing the sediment.

Store finished syrup in the refrigerator and use within 2 months.

Note- The average sap-to-syrup yield ratio is 40:1, meaning 10 gallons of sap would be required to make 1 quart of finished syrup.

Tapping sugar maples in the middle of the city! Homemade maple syrup can be done on a very small scale with minimal investment for maximum fun.

Turkey Brine
(Dry Brine and Wet Brine Methods)

I've had the pleasure of hosting Thanksgiving for my family at our little cabin in Northern Michigan every year since we bought it in 2011. Thanksgiving instnatly became the family's favorite holiday of the year. We managed to find a way to make the day relaxed and unfussy without sacrificing the important traditions along the way. Although we don't have TV signal to watch the Lions play, which is basically an unforgiveable sin in Michigan, but I'm at peace with it.

Over the years, I've tried many different methods for seasoning and brining the beloved bird in order to produce the most juicy Thanksgiving turkey imaginable. In my experience, brining is the way to go, no question. There are two different ways to brine though, wet and dry. I've had very good results with both, and recommend them highly. My favorite, however, is the dry brine. Dry brining uses less ingredients, less space, less work, less mess, and the roasted bird browns beautifully with crispy skin that is to die for.

DRY BRINE

3 tablespoons kosher salt
½ teaspoon dried thyme
½ teaspoon rubbed sage
½ teaspoon rosemary
1 tablespoon dark brown sugar

Combine ingredients in a small bowl. Rub into and under the skin of the bird. Place turkey on baking sheet or in roasting pan and refrigerate uncovered for 2-3 days.

WET BRINE

1-pound kosher salt   Boiling water
1-pound dark brown sugar   Large cooler
Two 7-pound bags of ice

Bring a large pot of water to a boil. Add kosher salt and brown sugar, stirring to combine. Continue stirring occasionally with pot of medium-high heat until dissolved. Remove from heat.

Fill clean cooler with ice. Pour salt/sugar mixture over ice and stir to combine. Add turkey (neck and bag of giblets removed) to the cooler. Close cooler lid securely and let sit 24 hours, turning turkey periodically. Before cooking, remove turkey from brine and pat dry with paper towel.

Let turkey come to room temperature, then roast or grill as desired.

MY LITTLE MICHIGAN KITCHEN

Apple Cider Vinaigrette

¼ cup apple cider

½ cup cider vinegar

1 teaspoon dry mustard

¼ teaspoon salt

¼ teaspoon freshly ground black pepper

Pinch of cinnamon

1 cup canola oil

Whisk together apple cider, cider vinegar, dry mustard, salt, pepper, and cinnamon in a medium bowl. Continue whisking while slowly drizzling oil into mixture. Continue whisking until very smooth and all ingredients are incorporated.

Keep refrigerated in an airtight container for up to 2 weeks.

Makes about 1½ cups.

Serve with Green Salad with Grilled Chicken, Apples, and Cranberries (Pg. 64)

Maple Syrup Vinaigrette

½ cup pure maple syrup

¼ cup balsamic vinegar

2 teaspoons Dijon mustard

½ teaspoon salt

½ teaspoon freshly ground black pepper

½ cup canola oil

In a medium bowl, whisk all ingredients together except the oil. Slowly drizzle in the oil, whisking constantly until combined thoroughly and dressing has a creamy appearance.

Keep refrigerated in an airtight container for up to 2 weeks.

Makes about 1 ½ cups.

Serve with Brussels Sprouts and Bacon Salad (Pg.60)

Riviera Dressing

1 cup canola oil

½ cup distilled white vinegar

1 cup granulated sugar

1 teaspoon dry mustard powder

1 teaspoons poppy seeds

Combine all ingredients in a medium bowl and whisk until creamy.

Keep refrigerated for up to 2 weeks.

Makes about 2 ½ cups.

Serve with Riviera Salad (Pg. 67)

Balsamic Glaze

2 cups Balsamic Vinegar

½ cup brown sugar

In a medium saucepan, heat balsamic vinegar and brown sugar over medium-low heat until sugar is dissolved. Simmer, stirring frequently, until liquid has reduced by half (about 20 minutes). Glaze should be thickened slightly and have a syrup-like consistency. It will thicken a bit more as it cools.

Let glaze cool, then store in a sealed container in the refrigerator until ready to use.

Balsamic Glaze can be prepared up to 1 week ahead of time.

Makes 2 cups.

Serve with Balsamic Glazed Carrots, (Pg. 82), Caprese Salad (Pg. 63)

Cherry Barbecue Sauce

1 cup frozen tart cherries

1 cup ketchup

½ cup brown sugar

1 tablespoon Worcestershire sauce

In a large saucepan, combine all ingredients and bring to a boil over medium-high heat, stirring frequently. Reduce heat to low and simmer, stirring frequently until thickened, about 30 minutes.

Transfer mixture to a blender and pulse until very smooth.

Makes about 2 cups.

Seal in an airtight container and store in refrigerator. Use within 4 weeks.

Fresh Tomato Salsa

A leisurely stroll through the Farmer's Market and a few minutes in the kitchen, and you've got better-than-restaurant-style salsa for your weekend enjoyment. Double dipping permitted.

¼ cup chopped red onion

5 or 6 ripe medium tomatoes, cut into pieces

¼ cup chopped fresh cilantro

1-2 jalapenos, seeded

1 clove garlic, chopped

Juice of ½ lime, plus more to taste

¼ teaspoon kosher salt, plus more to taste

Using an electric food processor, pulse the onion until very finely diced.

Add tomatoes, cilantro, jalapenos, and garlic. Pulse until chopped fine.

Stir in lime juice and salt. Adjust seasoning as desired.

Keep refrigerated for up to 4-6 days.

Hot Cherry Mustard

¼ cup dried mustard powder

¼ cup water

1 pound tart cherries, pitted

1 cup apple cider vinegar

½ cup honey

¼ cup brown sugar

Salt, to taste

In a small bowl, whisk together the mustard powder and water into a paste.

In a medium saucepan over medium heat, add cherries, cider vinegar, honey, and brown sugar. Bring to a boil and reduce heat to low, simmering until cherries are tender and liquid is syrupy, about 25 minutes.

Transfer all ingredients to a blender and pulse until very smooth. Add salt to taste.

Serve with pretzels.

Keep refrigerated in airtight container for up to 4 weeks.

Salsa Verde

1-pound fresh tomatillos, husked and rinsed

1 jalapeño, chopped fine

½ cup chopped onion

1 clove garlic, minced

1 ½ teaspoons kosher salt

2 tablespoons minced cilantro

2 cups water

In a medium saucepan, bring all ingredients to a boil, reduce heat to medium-low and simmer for 15 minutes, or until tomatillos are soft.

Transfer to food processor or blender and blend until almost smooth.

Let cool. Store in airtight container and keep refrigerated for up to 4-6 days.

Serve with tortilla chips or use in Salsa Verde Chicken Enchiladas (Recipe pg. 133)

Makes about 3 cups.

Ginger Syrup and Candied Ginger

1 cup water

1 cup plus 2 tablespoons granulated sugar, divided

1 cup fresh ginger, peeled and sliced very thin

Ginger Syrup-

Combine water, 1 cup sugar, and ginger in a heavy-bottomed saucepan over medium heat. Bring to a boil, then reduce heat to low and simmer for 30 minutes or until syrupy. Strain to remove ginger pieces. Do not discard. Allow syrup to cool completely, then store in the refrigerator in an airtight container for up to one month.

Candied Ginger:-

Arrange ginger pieces on a sheet of waxed paper to dry for 20 minutes. Sprinkle with 2 tablespoons sugar and toss to coat. Let dry completely before storing in an airtight container. Keep refrigerated for up to 3 months.

Serving suggestions:

Use in Ginger Sweet Tea, (Recipe pg.194)

Add to club soda for a homemade ginger ale.

Add to lemonade.

Drizzle over ice cream.

Make Ginger snow cones.

Candied ginger can help settle upset stomachs, particularly due to motion-sickness in my experience.

These sauces are some of my favorite additions to a special brunch or dessert. Served as a trio and they remind me of Neapolitan ice cream as a kid...only way better. Drizzle this goodness over waffles, pancakes, Monkey Bread, or ice cream. They also make perfect dipping sauces for Beignets or Cinnamon-Sugar Soft Pretzels.

Warm Vanilla Sauce

2 cups heavy cream

1 cup granulated sugar

2 tablespoons all-purpose flour

½ cup unsalted butter

1 ½ tablespoons pure vanilla extract

In a medium saucepan set over medium heat, whisk together the sugar, flour, and heavy cream. Add butter and heat until boiling, whisking frequently.

Let simmer for a few minutes until sauce has thickened to your desired consistency.

Remove from heat and stir in vanilla.

Keep warm until ready to serve.

Warm Nutella Sauce

⅓ cup Nutella

3 tablespoons heavy cream

Combine Nutella and heavy cream in a microwave-safe bowl. Microwave for 45-60 seconds, stirring every 15 seconds. Serve immediately.

Raspberry Coulis

1 ½ pounds fresh raspberries, about 6 cups

¼ cup granulated sugar

1 tablespoon lemon juice

Combine raspberries, sugar, and lemon juice in a medium heavy-bottomed saucepan over medium heat. Bring to a gentle boil, then reduce to a simmer, stirring frequently until raspberries break down, sugar dissolves, and sauce has thickened slightly about 5 minutes. Remove from heat and press sauce through a fine-mesh sieve to remove seeds. Cool to room temperature, then seal in airtight container and refrigerate. Sauce will thicken more as it cools.

Serve warm or chilled.

Pizza Sauce

This pizza sauce is my go-to for Detroit Deep Dish (Recipe pg. 121). Ready in 45 minutes and is made with ingredients I always have in my pantry makes for a win-win.

2 tablespoons extra-virgin olive oil

3 cloves garlic, minced

2 teaspoons dried oregano

Pinch of red pepper flakes

1 (28-ounce) can crushed tomatoes

1 teaspoon garlic powder

1 teaspoon onion powder

1 tablespoon brown sugar

Kosher salt, to taste

Heat olive oil in a heavy-bottomed saucepan set over medium heat. Add minced garlic, oregano, and red pepper flakes and heat for about 30 seconds until fragrant.

Add crushed tomatoes, garlic powder, onion powder, and brown sugar. Bring just to a boil, then reduce heat to maintain a simmer. Continue simmering for 30 minutes. Taste and season with salt.

Point Betsie Lighthouse- Frankfort, Michigan

Hot Fudge Sauce

2 cups heavy cream

4 tablespoons unsalted butter

½ cup brown sugar

¾ cup granulated sugar

¼ teaspoon fine sea salt

2 ounces bittersweet chocolate finely chopped

1 ¼ cups unsweeetened cocoa powder, sifted

½ teaspoon pure vanilla extract

In medium saucepan set over medium-low heat, combine cream, butter, sugars and salt. Bring to a simmer for 45 seconds. Add chopped chocolate, and whisk to dissolve. Turn off heat. Add cocoa, whisking until smooth.

Turn heat to low, and simmer sauce until glossy, whisking constantly, 20 seconds. Remove from heat, and stir in vanilla.

Serve warm over ice cream or Hot Fudge Cream Puffs (Recipe pg. 146).

"Always serve too much hot fudge sauce on hot fudge sundaes. It makes people overjoyed, and puts them in your debt."
–Judith Olney

Caramel-Banana Syrup

¼ cup (4 tablespoons) unsalted butter

½ cup light brown sugar

¼ cup water

2 bananas (fresh, not over-ripe), sliced ¼-inch thick

In a medium saucepan over medium heat, melt 4 tablespoons unsalted butter. Add brown sugar and water, and stir to combine.

Bring to a boil over medium-high heat, stirring frequently. Once boiling, cook for a minute or two until mixture has thickened somewhat and caramelized.

Once you've reached your desired consistency (for thicker syrup, just cook an extra 30 seconds or so), remove from heat and stir in vanilla and sliced bananas.

Serve immediately with pancakes, waffles, French Toast, or ice cream.

Buttermilk Ranch Dressing

While this homemade ranch dressing is perfectly suitable for your salad needs, the truly Michigan way of life is to dip everything in ranch. Veggies, chicken, hot wings, pizza. It's also great on a sandwich in lieu of mayonnaise.

1 cup buttermilk

1 cup mayonnaise

¾ cup sour cream

2 tablespoons lemon juice, more as needed

4 cloves garlic, minced

2 teaspoons minced fresh parsley

1 teaspoon minced fresh dill

½ teaspoon minced fresh chives

Pinch of cayenne pepper

½ teaspoon kosher salt

½ teaspoon freshly ground black pepper

In a large bowl, whisk all ingredients together until smooth. Taste and adjust amounts of lemon juice, salt, and pepper as needed.

Seal in an airtight container and keep refrigerated for up to 7 days.

Cheddar Cheese Sauce

Serve with Chicken Purses (Recipe pg. 116), Soft Pretzels (Recipe pg. 44), or Roasted Broccoli. (Pg. 90)

2 tablespoons unsalted butter

2 tablespoons all-purpose flour

1 cup whole milk, warmed

1 ½ cup shredded sharp cheddar cheese

Salt and pepper, to taste

Pinch of nutmeg

2-3 drops of hot sauce, optional

In a heavy-bottomed saucepan over medium heat, melt the butter. Add flour and whisk until smooth. Continue cooking flour for 30 seconds, stirring constantly. Gradually pour milk into butter mixture, stirring constantly. Continue cooking and stirring until thickened slightly but do not boil.

Add cheese, salt, pepper, nutmeg, and hot sauce, stirring to combine. Continue cooking until cheese has melted. Taste and adjust seasonings as desired. Serve warm.

Cinnamon-Honey Butter

½ cup (1 stick) unsalted butter, at room temperature

3 tablespoons honey

¼ teaspoon cinnamon

⅛ teaspoon kosher salt

In the bowl of a stand mixer fitted with the paddle attachment, combine all ingredients and beat at medium speed until smooth.

Serve at room temperature.

Serving suggestions-

Fluffy Buttermilk Biscuits (Pg. 41)

Oatmeal Buttermilk Pancakes (Pg. 44)

Potato Rolls (Pg. 50)

Sour Cream Waffles (Pg.20)

Homemade Marshmallows, pg. 236

Basics

All-Butter Pie Crust

Yield: 2 pie crusts

2 ½ cups (315 grams) all-purpose flour

1 tablespoon (15 grams) granulated sugar (Omit sugar if using in a savory recipe.)

1 teaspoon (5 grams) salt

2 sticks (8 ounces/225 grams) unsalted butter, cubed and very cold

1 cup water with ice

Cube the butter and set in freezer for 5 minutes while you measure the remaining ingredients.

In a large bowl, whisk together the flour, sugar, and salt.

Add butter to the flour mixture and combine with a fork, two butter knives, or a pastry blender. Be sure not to mix the butter in completely. Some visible bits of butter should remain, no larger than the size of a pea.

Drizzle ½ cup of the cold water over the mixture, and bring the dough together using a rubber spatula. Add more water, one tablespoon at a time, as needed to bring the dough together. You shouldn't need to use more than ¾ cup water.

Bring the dough together into a ball by hand, and divide in half. Shape into discs.

Wrap each disc in plastic wrap and refrigerate for 2 hours before rolling dough out.

-HOW TO BLIND BAKE A PIE CRUST-

Place pie crust into pie pan and crimp the edges as desired. Line the crust with aluminum foil, then fill at least ⅔ full with pie weights (dried beans or rice work well.) Chill crust for at least 30 minutes.

Bake at 375°F for 20 minutes* or until edges of crust are golden. Remove pan from oven and gently lift out the pie weights and foil. Prick the bottom of the crust with a fork a few times and return to oven for an additional 15 to 20 minutes until lightly golden.

Let cool completely before filling.

*For Deep Dish Quiche, increase intital blind bake time to 30-40 minutes.

**This process is also referred to as "par-baking".

Hot Water Crust

*Hot Water Crust is a very forgiving homemade pie crust that is well-suited for savory applications, such as UP North Pasties, Chicken Purses, or Chicken Pot Pie. This is a great crust to practice with if you're not confident with making homemade crusts because it rolls out **beautifully**.*

Half Batch-

¾ cups shortening or lard

¾ cups boiling water

2 ¼ cups all-purpose flour

¾ teaspoon salt

Full Batch-

1 ½ cups shortening or lard

1 ½ cups boiling water

4 ½ cups all-purpose flour

1 ½ teaspoons salt

In a medium bowl, combine the shortening and boiling water and stir until melted. Add flour and salt and mix until combined. Cover with plastic wrap and chill in refrigerator for 2 hours.

How to Prevent a Bundt® Cake from Sticking to Pan

If you've ever had a Bundt® cake get stuck in the pan, you know how frustrating that can be. Here are a few tips to set you up for success or to troubleshoot for the future. If your cake does stick to the pan though, not to worry. Gently patch it back together and make a double batch of icing to cover the imperfections. Serve cheerfully and never apologize.

- Try using vegetable oil spray or melted shortening instead of butter.

- If using flour, be very generous but tap out excess. For chocolate cakes, use cocoa powder instead.

- Always use a nonstick pan with no scratches. Recommended: NordicWare 50342 ProForm Bundt Pan with Handles, 12 Cup. Very inexpensive and performs very well.

- Use pastry brush to spread oil/shortening into all areas of the pan's design

- Coat the pan immediately prior to filling with batter. Not when you start preheating the oven.

- Gently loosen the edges of the cake from the pan with a soft spatula. Be sure to slide it down as far as you can, and don't forget to do the same for the center tube portion of the pan as well.

- Let warm cake rest several minutes before removing from pan. 10-15 minutes before flipping the pan upside-down over a cooling rack. Let cool a few minutes upside down. If cake does not release itself from the pan with only a few gentle nudges in this time, pop it back in the cooling oven for a few minutes to help soften any baked on areas.

- Brush pan with homemade Pan Release. Recipe below.

Pan Release

¼ cup canola oil

¼ cup vegetable shortening

¼ cup all-purpose flour

Whisk or blend ingredients until smooth. Apply to baking dishes with a pastry brush to prevent cakes from sticking.

Store leftover Pan Release in an airtight contained in the refrigerator for up to 6 weeks. Let come to room temperature to ensure spreadable consistency.

Grand Rapids. Michigan

Beef Jerky

Beef Jerky is one of those things that are very expensive to buy, but so easy to make at home for much less, plus you've got control over the flavor and spiciness level to suit your own tastes. I'm fairly certain that if need be, my husband would gladly survive on homemade beef jerky and cereal. This is the perfect snack to enjoy when we're hiking on one of our favorite trails.

2 pounds boneless top or bottom round beef roast

½ cup Worcestershire sauce

½ cup low-sodium soy sauce

½ cup pure maple syrup

½-1 teaspoon hickory liquid smoke, adjust to taste

1 teaspoon freshly ground black pepper

¼ teaspoon cayenne pepper, adjust to taste

Place beef in freezer for a few hours before slicing. This helps the meat to hold its shape and makes it easier to slice very thin and evenly.

Slice beef into even slices, about ¼" thick.

Combine Worcestershire, soy sauce, maple syrup, liquid smoke, black pepper, and cayenne pepper in a large zipper storage bag. Add sliced beef to bag and seal bag tightly. Turn bag a few times to ensure that beef is coated evenly.

Refrigerate 12-18 hours to allow flavors to marinate.

Oven or dehydrator method-

Preheat oven to 170°F, or a dehydrator to 160°.

Arrange sliced beef in a single layer on a wire cooling rack and place on center shelf in oven. Set a rimmed baking sheet on lower oven rack to catch any drips.

Dehydrate in oven or dehydrator for 1 ½-3 hours, checking regularly. Jerky is done when it bends slightly before breaking. If it feels moist to the touch or bends easily, it needs more time. If it snaps when bent, it is overdone.

Let cool completely before sealing in zipper storage bag with air removed. Can be kept at room temperature for up to 1 week, in refrigerator for up to one month, or freezer for up to 3 months.

Homemade Marshmallows

Make these marshmallows once and you'll have a hard time enjoying store-bought again. The texture and flavor are so much more pure and delicate, and they toast beautifully for s'mores or on top of sweet potatoes.

0.75-ounces (3 envelopes) unflavored gelatin

1 cup cold water, divided

1 ½ cups granulated sugar

1 cup light corn syrup

¼ teaspoon kosher salt

1 teaspoon pure vanilla extract

¼ cup confectioners' sugar

¼ cup cornstarch

In the bowl of a stand mixer fitted with the whisk attachment, mix gelatin and ½ cup of the cold water just until combined.

In a small saucepan with candy thermometer attached, combine remaining ½ cup water, sugar, corn syrup, and salt. Heat over medium heat, whisking frequently, until mixture reaches 240°F, about 10 minutes.

Remove from heat. Turn mixer on low speed and very gradually drizzle sugar mixture into bowl with gelatin. Raise speed to high and mix until very, very thick and lukewarm. This will take about 15 minutes. Add vanilla, then mix again until thoroughly combined.

In a small bowl, whisk together the confectioners' sugar and cornstarch.

Spray a 9×13-inch baking pan with cooking spray. Sprinkle pan generously with cornstarch mixture. Set remaining mixture aside to use later.

Spray a silicone spatula with cooking spray and spread marshmallow mixture into pan. Dust top of marshmallow mixture with some more of the cornstarch mixture. Set aside remaining cornstarch mixture.

Let marshmallow set at room temperature, uncovered, for 8-24 hours. Overnight works great.

Once marshmallow has set, turn pan over onto a cutting board to remove the marshmallow. It should come out easily. Using a very sharp knife, cut marshmallows into the size and shape you desire, dusting the cut sides with remaining cornstarch mixture. Lightly oil knife blade if needed.

Store in airtight container at room temperature.

Maple-Cinnamon Pecan Granola

¾ cup pure maple syrup (Grade B or Grade A dark amber)

½ cup unsalted butter, melted

3 cups old-fashioned oats

1 cup chopped pecans

1 cup coconut flakes

½ teaspoon ground cinnamon

Pinch of sea salt

1 ½ cups dried cherries, optional

Preheat oven to 300°F.

In a large mixing bowl, combine maple syrup, butter, oats, pecans, coconut, cinnamon, and salt.

Spread on rimmed baking sheet.

Bake at 300°F for 40 minutes, stirring occasionally, until golden. If using dried cherries, add them in the last 10 minutes of baking time.

Let cool completely before transferring to an airtight container for storage. For best results, enjoy within 2 weeks.

Michigan Cure-All

If you happen to find yourself in Michigan and you're suffering from an ailment or illness of any kind, do as Michiganders do.

P.S. It's called POP. Not soda.

Ingredients:

Vernors. Absolutely no substitutions. Very very cold. Preferably from a can that has been stashed in the coldest part of the refrigerator for just such an occasion.

Cubed ice, or none at all. This is improtant. Crushed ice melts too quickly and comprimises the integrity of the carbonation. You've got to trust me on this one. For best results, skip the ice altogether.

An insulated cup. If available, a handle is a nice feature.

Straw, optional.

Directions:

Pre-cool the cup by filling with cold water and letting sit a few minutes. Pour out water and dry cup.

Add ice, if desired.

Gradually pour cold Vernors into the cup, allowing the fizz to subside before topping off.

If cup is not insulated, a coaster or napkin may be necessary.

Find the comfiest chair, couch, or bed in the house. Don your finest sweatpants.

Sip the Cure-All slowly and frequently.

Re-administer as needed until no symptoms remain.

-HOW TO SPATCHCOCK A CHICKEN (OR TURKEY)-

What's a spatchcock, you might ask? To spatchcock a chicken simply means to remove the backbone so that you can lay the chicken flat for cooking purposes. This method is much easier than you might think, and it allows for a magnificently grilled chicken that cooks very nicely and much more evenly than if you were to leave the bird whole. It's basically a butterflied whole chicken. All you need is a whole chicken and a pair of heavy duty kitchen shears.

1. Lay the whole bird breast-side down on a work surface. (I recommend a rimmed baking sheet to catch the juices.)

2. Feel for the backbone and using kitchen shears, make two cuts the entire length of the chicken on either side of the backbone. You'll be removing about a 1-inch strip down the center of the back of the bird.

3. Turn the chicken over and press down on the breastbone to flatten out the chicken. That's it! You officially know how to spatchcock a chicken.

Tips for Buying a Fresh Whole Fish

If you aren't able to catch your own fish fresh from the river, it is important to know what to look for when purchasing a whole fish for cooking.

1. Smell it.

Fresh fish do not smell like fish. They should smell like the sea/lake/river- sort of the smell of briny water. If it smells fishy, it is not fresh and you should not buy it.

2. Look at the eyes.

The eyes should be clear and bright, not dull and cloudy. They should also look a little bit bulged.

3. Look at the skin/scales.

The surface of the fish should feel firm when pressed, and look shiny, bright, and metallic. If it looks patchy, dull, or discolored, it has seen better days.

4. Check the gills.

Gills of a freshly caught fish are bright red and wet-looking, not dark burgundy red or dry or slimy.

...In other words, a fresh fish should look like it is alive.

"Michigan, with its delicious American name.
How lucky one must be to live there."

–Gary Shteyngart

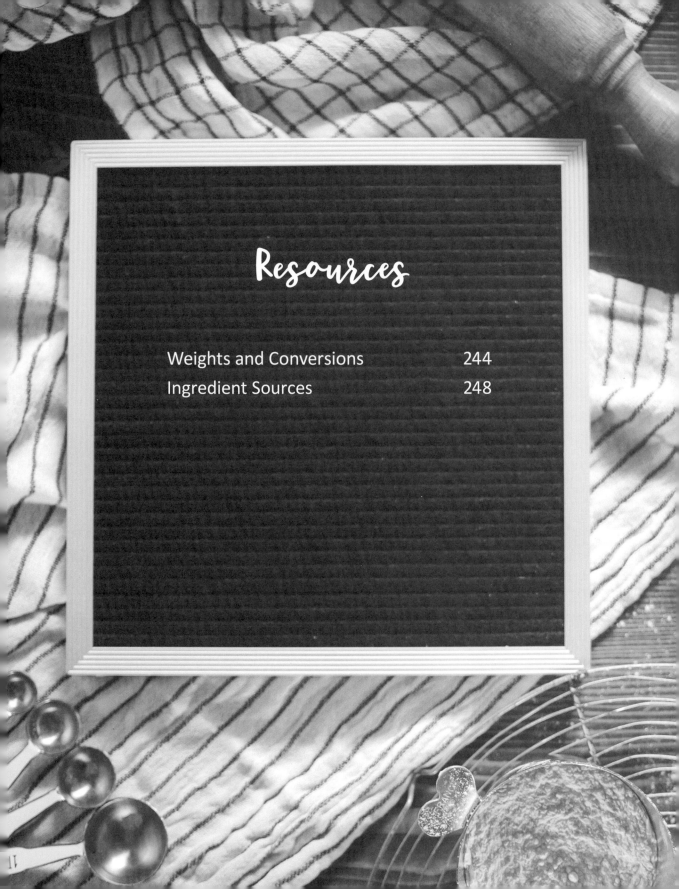

Resources

WEIGHTS AND CONVERSIONS

Temperature Conversions

Fahrenheit	Celsius
475°	245°
450°	230°
425°	220°
400°	200°
375°	190°
350°	180°
325°	165°
300°	150°
275°	135°

Ounces to Grams

¼ oz	7 g	5 oz	150 g	11 oz	325 g
½ oz	15 g	6 oz	175 g	12 oz	340 g
1 oz	30 g	7 oz	200 g	13 oz	375 g
2 oz	55 g	8 oz	225 g	14 oz	400 g
3 oz	86 g	9 oz	250 g	15 oz	425 g
4 oz	115 g	10 oz	300 g	16 oz (1lb)	455 g

All-Purpose Flour

1 teaspoon	3 g
1 tablespoon	8 g
¼ cup	31 g
⅓ cup	42 g
½ cup	63 g
⅔ cup	83 g
¾ cup	94 g
1 cup	125 g

Bread Flour

1 teaspoon	3 g
1 tablespoon	8 g
¼ cup	32 g
⅓ cup	42 g
½ cup	64 g
⅔ cup	85 g
¾ cup	95 g
1 cup	127 g

Baking Powder

1 teaspoon	5 g
1 tablespoon	15 g

Baking Soda

1 teaspoon	5 g
1 tablespoon	15 g

Cornstarch

1 teaspoon	3 g
1 tablespoon	8 g

Instant Yeast

1 teaspoon	3 g
1 tablespoon	9 g
One packet (2 ½ teaspoons)	7 g

Kosher Salt

1 teaspoon	3 g
1 tablespoon	9 g

Table Salt

1 teaspoon	6 g
1 tablespoon	18 g

Extracts

1 teaspoon	4 g
1 tablespoon	13 g

Brown Sugar, packed

1 teaspoon	5 g
1 tablespoon	14 g
⅛ cup	28 g
¼ cup	55 g
⅓ cup	73 g
½ cup	110 g
⅔ cup	147 g
¾ cup	165 g
1 cup	220 g

Confectioners' Sugar

1 teaspoon	2 g
1 tablespoon	7 g
⅛ cup	15 g
¼ cup	30 g
⅓ cup	40 g
½ cup	60 g
⅔ cup	80 g
¾ cup	90 g
1 cup	120 g

Butter/Shortening/Lard

1 teaspoon	5 g
1 tablespoon	14 g
¼ cup	57 g
½ cup (1 stick)	113 g
¾ cup	170 g
1 cup (2 sticks)	227 g

Syrups (Honey, Corn Syrup, Maple Syrup, Molasses)

1 teaspoon	7 g
1 tablespoon	21 g
¼ cup	85 g
⅓ cup	113 g
½ cup	170 g
⅔ cup	226 g
¾ cup	255 g
1 cup	336 g

Granulated Sugar

1 teaspoon	4 g
1 tablespoon	12 g
⅛ cup	25 g
¼ cup	50 g
⅓ cup	67 g
½ cup	100 g
⅔ cup	133 g
¾ cup	150 g
1 cup	200 g

Canola/Vegetable/Olive Oil

1 teaspoon	5 g
1 tablespoon	14 g
¼ cup	56 g
⅓ cup	75 g
½ cup	111 g
⅔ cup	149 g
¾ cup	168 g
1 cup	224 g

Old-Fashioned Oats

1 teaspoon	2 g
1 tablespoon	5 g
⅛ cup	10 g
¼ cup	20 g
⅓ cup	27 g
½ cup	40 g
⅔ cup	53 g
¾ cup	60 g
1 cup	80 g

Whole Nuts

¼ cup	36 g
⅓ cup	45 g
½ cup	71 g
⅔ cup	79 g
¾ cup	106 g
1 cup	142 g

Milk/Sour Cream/Yogurt/Buttermilk/Heavy Cream

1 teaspoon	5 g
1 tablespoon	15 g
¼ cup	60 g
⅓ cup	80 g
½ cup	120 g
⅔ cup	160 g
¾ cup	180 g
1 cup	240 g

Chocolate Chips

¼ cup	43 g
⅓ cup	57 g
½ cup	85 g
⅔ cup	113 g
¾ cup	128 g
1 cup	170 g

Cocoa Powder

1 teaspoon	2 g
1 tablespoon	5 g
¼ cup	21 g
⅓ cup	25 g
½ cup	43 g
⅔ cup	50 g
¾ cup	64 g
1 cup	85 g

Cream Cheese/Ricotta

1 teaspoon	5 g
1 tablespoon	14 g
¼ cup	56 g
⅓ cup	75 g
½ cup	112 g
⅔ cup	150 g
¾ cup	169 g
1 cup	225 g

Chopped/Slivered Nuts

¼ cup	28 g
⅓ cup	38 g
½ cup	57 g
⅔ cup	75 g
¾ cup	85 g
1 cup	113 g

Crushed Pineapple, drained

¼ cup	50 g
⅓ cup	67 g
½ cup	100 g
⅔ cup	133 g
¾ cup	150 g
1 cup	200 g

Pumpkin Puree

¼ cup	61 g
⅓ cup	81 g
½ cup	122 g
⅔ cup	162 g
¾ cup	183 g
1 cup	244 g

-INGREDIENT SOURCES-

If your local grocery store does not carry a particular ingredient needed for a recipe, most are available online. Here is the information for some of the items that may be difficult to find in some stores.

Stubb's Hickory Liquid Smoke- Amazon.com

Wisconsin Brick Cheese- Widemer's Cheese Cellars
www.widmerscheese.com/product/foil-pack-aged-brick-14-ounces/

Vietnamese Cinnamon - Penzey's Spices
www.penzeys.com/online-catalog/vietnamese-cinnamon-ground/c-24/p-955/pd-s

Homebrew Old Fashioned Root Beer Soda Pop Base - Adventures in Homebrewing
www.homebrewing.org/

Brewing Yeast - Adventures in Homebrewing
www.homebrewing.org/Coopers-15-gram-Yeast_p_5247.html

Almond Paste- Solo Almond Paste- 8oz. box.
Available on Amazon.com and Walmart, in store and online.

Tapioca Starch/Tapioca flour- Bob's Red Mill
www.bobsredmill.com/tapioca-flour.html

Vernors Ginger Ale- Available on Amazon.com

Smoked Whitefish-*www.bearcatsfish.com/product/smoked-whitefish/*

Detroit Pizza Pan- Lloyd Pans
lloydpans.com/pizza-tools/regional-style-pizza-pans/detroit-style-pizza-pans

Michigan Maple Syrup- *michiganmaplefarms.com, harwoodgold.com*

Frozen Tart Pie Cherries- *www.kingorchards.com/product/frozen-michigan-tart-cherries/*

Dried Cherries- *www.brownwoodacres.com/dried-tart-cherries/*

Dried Mushrooms- *www.earthy.com/Dried-Mushrooms-C29.aspx*

The G-Rap Map

Robin, Michigan's State Bird

Index

Recipe Index

THANKSGIVING FAVORITES

Grilled Whole Turkey, 126

Turkey Brine, Wet and Dry, 204

Sweet Potato Casserole with

> Toasted Marshmallows, 94, *95*

Salted Maple Pie, 156, *157*

Roasted Butternut Squash Soup, 77

Brussels Sprout and Bacon Salad, 60

Jellied Cranberry Sauce, *86*, 87

Balsamic Glazed Carrots, 82

Creamy Mashed Red Potatoes, 88, *89*

Potato Rolls, 50, *51*

Cinnamon-Honey Butter, 225

Apple Cider Sangria, 192, *193*

Dutch Apple Pie, 150, *151*

About the Author

Mandy McGovern is the creator, recipe developer, and photographer of Kitchen Joy. Her unwavering love for Julia Child and collecting cookbooks prompted her to create her blog in 2013. Her site has since provided millions of readers with tried and true recipes and techniques based on her belief that homemade is better than store bought. She compulsively cooks and bakes in her little Michigan kitchen surrounded by her husband and their two daughters.

Visit Mandy at kitchenjoyblog.com, or connect on Instagram (@kitchenjoy).

*"make it your ambition to lead a quiet life:
To mind your own business and work with your hands"*

1 Thessalonians 4:11-12

Gratitude

Michael. My rock. My hero. My deepest love. You make me smile when the skies are pitch black. Your encouragement and support has been an inspiration. Your shared interest in food, blogging, photography, travel, and everything else is something I cherish deeply. There's no one I would rather live life with and grow old alongside. Thank you for showing me what it is to be a loyal husband, and an honorable man. You are my everything.

Addilyn Joy. What can I say? You made me a Mama. From day one, we were a fun little duo. We have had countless adventures together already, and you're only two years old. Being your Mama is my greatest source of joy. I can't wait to be your biggest cheerleader as you grow and chase after your dreams. Dream big, sweet girl. You're going to do amazing things.

Amelia Joy. Our missing piece. You light up our home with your smile. You are the sweetest little sister Addilyn could have ever hoped for. You've been a fighter since before we met you, and we can't wait to watch how you use your strength for good as you grow. Being your Mama is my greatest source of joy and I'm so proud to call you my daughter.

Luke. My brother who has been by my side through thick, thin, and thinner. Who has seen me on my best days and my not-so-good days. You may be younger than me, but I look up to you more than almost anyone I've ever known. You are a shining example of overcoming obstacles and never giving up on your dreams. You're an incredibly hard worker with an unbelievable ability to master whichever field of study you find interesting at any given time. You give me courage to try new things and to chase my dreams. Thank you for all of your interest and encouragement throughout the cookbook process.

Mom. You wore so many hats in my life. Mom. Friend. Teacher. Short order cook. Taxi driver. Seamstress. Single-mother. Working mother. Fighter. Survivor. Supporter. Grandma. Mom, you have been so many things to me, and I'm so proud to be your daughter.

Robin L. Smith. Landscape Photographer and collaborator. Aunt and friend. Best neighbor ever. Don't lose me Robin.

Alex Rathbun, photographer and creator of Brightly Alex.(brightlyalex.com) Thank you for capturing me in my element. Your vision, attention to detail, and commitment to authenticity and style is such a gift. Keep chasing your dreams and sharing your talent with the world.

Julia Child. The fearless woman who changed home cooking forever. Her tenacity, vigor, and relentless pursuit for food knowledge have truly impacted my life immensely.

Deb Perelman, Smitten Kitchen. One of the very first food blogs I ever visited, and I was immediately hooked. Her creativity, writing, and approachable authenticity have truly inspired me.

The Yellow Table. When I started seriously researching the cookbook writing process, the story of Anna Watson Carl's cookbook journey and her excitement throughout the process was utterly contagious.

David Lebovitz. Food blogger, Cookbook Author, and Francophile. Could there be a better combo? I think not. To say that I am smitten with his work would be an understatement.

Recipe Testers- Lyndsey Friedt, Missie McGovern, Melanie Richardson, Kade Roggentine, Kayla Roggentine, Garrett Goodwin, Lauren Vermilye, Taryn Brenneman, Kim Dietlin, Michael McGovern, Katrina M. White, Gail Duhon, Kimmi Sparkman, Pam Kryger, Ruth Oltz

My Tribe. Lyndsey, Jodi, Melanie, Missie. You guys play along with my hair-brained ideas and support my wild dreams with open minds and cheerful hearts. You're better than Google for parenting or weather advice. I cherish each of you deeply. A million thanks.

Melissa. The sunflowers are for you, girl. You'll never be forgotten.

My blog readers. The fact that anyone spends their time visiting my site is such a dream come true for me. I am so thankful for all those who have supported Kitchen Joy over the years. It means the world to me.

Siciliano's Market for their beer and wine recommendations, great selections, and endless knowledge. www.sicilianosmkt.com

The Plainfield branch of the Kent District Library. My oasis for writing and editing this book. I loved my weekly solo library dates. Maybe someday a copy of this book will grace their shelves.

The following books were invaluable resources to me througout the process of learning how to write and self-publish this cookbook.

Book Design Made Simple: A step-by-step guide to designing and typesetting your own book using Adobe® InDesign® by Fiona Raven & Glenna Collett, second edition, 2017.

Adobe InDesignCC 2017 Release Classroom In A Book®: The official training workbook from Adobe by Kelly Kordes Anton and John Cruise

The Recipe Writer's Handbook, Revised and Expanded by Barbara Gibbs Ostmann and Jane L. Baker, Houghton Mifflin Harcourt; 1 edition (March 30, 2001)

The Baker's Appendix: The Essential Kitchen Companion, with Deliciously Dependable, Infinitely Adaptable Recipes by Jessica Reed, Clarkson Potter (March 21, 2017)

Will Write for Food: The Complete Guide to Writing Cookbooks, Blogs, Memoir, Recipes, and More by Dianne Jacob, Da Capo Lifelong Books; 3 edition (July 14, 2015)

Last, but certainly not least. My home. When we were house shopping, when we walked into this house after several other houses just weren't the right fit, we just knew it. We sat on the couch and said it felt like home and that we didn't want to leave. I immediately knew that this was the stage for the rest of our lives. This would be where our family grew to completion. This would be where our daughters learned to walk, talk, read, love, grow, dream, and achieve. This would be where we gathered together for occasions both happy and sad. Where we would carve out time as a family on Sunday evenings to unwind together before a new week begins. Where we would lay our heads every single night under the same roof together, waking to new mercies every morning. Where we would strive to simplify, both in spirit and stuff. Where we would create meaningful moments with intention. Where we would make waffles on overcast Michigan Spring mornings with the first batch of the year's maple syrup. Where we would enjoy decorating Christmas cookies around the farmhouse table while the fireplace crackles in the background. Where Mama would scrub the walls with a bittersweet heart to remove the tiny handprints from peanut butter, crayons, and various other unidentifiable sources. Where we spilled more milk and coffee than seems humanly possible. Where we make snow angels, maple snow taffy, and track freezing cold toes into the house to warm up by the fire. This house would be where we truly and actively live our very best life with intention and full hearts.